"The Trinity has rightly come in for sustained attention over the past few decades, as theologians have relearned what we had nearly forgotten, namely, that the Trinity is the ground and grammar of all theology. It is now time for high Trinitarian theology to be translated into language for the churches, and that is what Sawyer is doing in this book. In simple language he explains complex realities and shows why the doctrine of the Trinity is deeply relational and issues out of and then back into rich and intimate worship."

—**Myk Habets**, Dean of Faculty, Head of Carey Graduate School, and Lecturer in Systematic Theology, Carey Baptist College (New Zealand)

"Sawyer presents a very lively account of the Trinity, not as abstract theology, but as an explanation of how the one God is the Father, the Son, and the Holy Spirit, three divine persons. He has read widely, writes eloquently, and constantly interacts with modern culture. I was pleased to see he rejects any hierarchical ordering in the Trinity, affirming unambiguously that the three persons are 'co-equal' God, as the Athanasian Creed asserts."

—**Kevin Giles**, author of *The Eternal Generation of the Son: Maintaining Orthodoxy in Trinitarian Theology*

"Without a doubt, although Trinitarian discussions abound in the academia today, the doctrine of the Trinity remains to be highly misunderstood, consciously marginalized, and ignorantly unappreciated by many Christians in the local church. Sawyer makes a passionate appeal to give the doctrine of the Trinity a chance. By intentionally looking at it, he asserts, we will come to appreciate its internal splendor and its many personal, soteriological, and missional implications. Sawyer invites us to prepare ourselves to be dazzled by a beauty that our eyes often fail to notice. *Resurrecting the Trinity* addresses the most common (mis)understandings and answers the most common questions related to the doctrine. The book's practical approach makes it like a Trinitarian FAQ page."

—**Dick O. Eugenio**, Associate Professor of Theology at Asia-Pacific Nazarene Theological Seminary, Philippines

"This is an important work of spiritual theology. Sawyer deftly integrates historical and systematic theology with sound exegesis and relevant cultural references, making the overall work a pleasant read, albeit one requiring focused attention. I heartily recommend this work for colleges and seminaries, pastors committed to deeper discipleship in their congregations and any thoughtful believer who wonders why there is such a gap between official theology and everyday spiritualty. "

—**Charlie E. Self**, Professor of Church History,
The Assemblies of God Theological Seminary

"I highly commend this fascinating and highly relevant contribution to Trinitarian studies, applicable both to the theologically initiated, and those less familiar. Eager readers, no matter their background, will gain both theological insight and spiritual encouragement."

—**Eric Sorenson**, Pastor of Christian Formation,
Community Covenant Church, Santa Barbara, CA

"Sawyer's theologically meaty book is not for the fainthearted. Sawyer means to confront modern misconceptions about God, ones which cut across numerous denominational lines. In his own words, 'Failure to come to grips with the Trinity as persons in eternal self-giving relationships of love is perhaps the greatest failure of the Western church.' Sawyer tackles this problem head-on, digging into Scripture with the help of early church fathers and theologians. *Resurrecting the Trinity* is a helpful introduction to nuances in Trinitarian thought for the serious Christian reader."

—**Victor Kuligin**, Academic Dean and Lecturer,
Bible Institute of South Africa

"To paraphrase Augustine, nothing is as arduous, adventurous, or advantageous as grappling with the Trinity. In this spirit, we vigorously go to the mat for the reasonableness of the doctrine. But frequently we get tied in knots when wrestling with its ramifications for life. With careful instruction and insightful cues, Sawyer ingrains in us a Trinitarian reflex that will strain every sinew of our worship, work, and walk. Indeed, he pushes us to constantly and comprehensively maneuver as one with the Three-in-One."

—**J. Ed Komoszewski**, coauthor, *Reinventing Jesus* and
Putting Jesus in His Place

"This book is a prophetic call for the church to recover orthodoxy via orthopraxis but abandoning the cliché and the novel in Christianity. How the church does will depend on whether she is willing to heed this call. Getting our God out of our idolatrous box will be a tall task, but it is well worth it."

— **Sam Tsang**, Associate Professor, Hong Kong Baptist Theological Seminary; Adjunct Professor, Ambrose University College (Canada)

"Sawyer calls on a return to the doctrine of the Trinity as the theological root of all other Christian doctrines and as its unifying foundation. He effectively exposes the danger of any expression or belief—direct or indirect—that sees no relevance for this doctrine. The book is rich with the historical development of Trinitarian Christian thought, and shows how erroneous theologians, having conceived God in their fallen imaginations, have dangerously made their theological systems their theological methods. Sawyer's book is a welcome contribution to help recover any unfortunate disregard for the Trinity."

—**Imad N. Shehadeh**, President and Professor of Theology, Jordan Evangelical Theological Seminary

"This book explains the Trinity from a base of scholarly work in the Bible and historical theology, but makes it real through his own experience along with examples from movies and stories. I appreciated very much both the theological and relational emphases in the book."

—**David Owen**, President, Professor of Old Testament, Pacific Islands University (Guam)

Resurrecting the Trinity: A Plea to Recover the Wonder and Meaning of the Triune God

© 2017 by M. James Sawyer

Lexham Press, 1313 Commercial St., Bellingham, WA 98225
LexhamPress.com

First edition by Weaver Book Company.

Print ISBN 9781683591504
Digital ISBN 9781683591511

Cover design: Frank Gutbrod
Interior design: Nicholas Richardson
Editorial: Line for Line Publishing Services

Resurrecting the Trinity

A Plea to Recover the Wonder and Meaning of the Triune God

M. James Sawyer

LEXHAM PRESS

To George & Nancy

Contents

Foreword

Why does the Trinity even matter? Isn't it a mystery beyond human understanding? Who am I to think that I could possibly figure out God? These are honest and important questions. Let me ask a few questions that will tell you my answer. What if we could see what Jesus sees? What if we could know what he knows, and feel what he feels as he gazes into his Father's eyes? Scripture says that Jesus is sitting at the right hand of God the Father and lives in face-to-face intimacy with him in the Spirit. Have you ever thought about that? What if we could sit with Jesus? What if we could have Jesus' mind, share in his faith, love with his love, care with his heart in the Spirit? What if we could be a part of his relationship with his Father, and of his own anointing in the Holy Spirit?

For me, it is right here that we see the importance of the blessed Trinity and of all of the debates and fights of theological history. If Jesus is not the eternal Son of God then we are on our own to know God. But since Jesus is the eternal and beloved Son who knows his Father and shares abounding life with him in the Holy Spirit, and since the Father's Son became one of us, then new and staggering possibilities stare us in the face.

Allow me to share my favorite story as an illustration. On a Saturday afternoon more than twenty years ago, I was sitting on my couch in the den sorting through junk mail waiting to watch a football game on TV. I noticed movement to my far right near the floor. I turned to see my son and one of his buddies in stealth mode, low to the floor. They were decked out in camouflage, face paint, plastic guns and knives and helmets. Before I knew what was happening, two screaming camouflage blurs were flying through the air right at me as if shot out of a canon. The attack was on. For ten minutes or so there were mock explosions,

9

and machine gun fire and fights and wounds and deaths and resurrec-
tions before the three of us ended up in a pile of laughter on the floor.
Kneeling and trying to catch my breath, I heard this statement in my
mind: "Baxter, this is important, pay attention."

I had no idea what the message meant. After all, it was Saturday, a
dad and his boy and his friend were playing army on the floor of the
den. Surely there is nothing extraordinary about that. Something very
much like it happens every day around our world. The first clue came
when I realized that I actually did not know this other little boy at all.
I had never seen him, and didn't even know his name. Suppose that he
had appeared in the den alone. Suppose my son was in the back room
with his sisters and our dog Nessie. Presumably the little boy would
have known that I was Mr. Kruger, but that is about as far as things
would have gone. Not in a million years would he have come flying
through the air at me, not by himself.

He did not know me. He did not know what I was like, or what my
reaction would be. But my son did. And that was my second clue. My
son knows me. He knows that I love him, that he is one of the apples
of my eye. He knows that I *like* him and that he is always welcome and
wanted. So he did the most natural thing in the world. In the freedom
of knowing my heart, he ran to me to play. The miracle was that his
buddy was right in the middle of it all. Without even knowing what I
was seeing, I saw my son's relationship with me, his at-homeness and
freedom with me, go inside that other little boy. And he got to see with
my son's eyes, and feel with his heart, and play in his freedom with me.
He got to experience our fellowship. Our life became as much his as it
was ours.

It took my breath away when I realized what happened. I had been
given eyes to see what is—the gospel. The staggering truth of all truths
was played out for me to see.

Stop for a moment and take this in. This is the real gospel: Jesus has
included us in his own relationship and fellowship and life with his
Father in the Spirit. Who doesn't want to be right in the middle of such
a relationship, sharing in all that Jesus is and has and experiences with
his Father in the Holy Spirit? Why have few of us ever heard of such
a possibility? Why haven't we been taught this as truth and guided to
"abide in me" as Jesus commands from the first day of Sunday school?

My one-word answer is "mindset." Ideas shape what we see and what we don't. Wrong ideas keep us from seeing (and from experiencing) what is. And here is why I love Jim Sawyer and this book, *Resurrecting the Trinity*, in particular.

Theology serves the heart and its quest to share in Jesus' life or it proves itself nothing more than faddish intellectual entertainment. In this book you will feel Jim's heart as he harnesses his considerable mind and his mastery of history to help us see how we got so far from the truth of all truths. At points you will sense his frustration with the problem, and his own and our ineptitude, but he faints not. I love that. Like Jacob of old, Jim will not let go until the blessing arrives. He will take you on a historical drive through the centuries of Christian thought. Stay in the seat. Take notes. Raise questions. Behold. Dr. Sawyer knows where he is going and what he is talking about. He is after our enemy, our "mindset," our Western mindset, not for the sake of being disturbing (though he is not shy about that), but so that we can have better eyes. *Resurrecting the Trinity* is a wonderful gift to the human race, serving our heart's inconsolable longing to know Jesus and his Father, and to live in the world of the Holy Spirit.

—**C. Baxter Kruger,** Ph.D., author of
The Shack Revisited and *Patmos*

Preface

While I studied the doctrine of the Trinity both in college and seminary and have in that sense always been Trinitarian, the Trinity was not at the center of my theological understanding.

The prominence of the Trinity first caught my attention in the early 90s during the widely reported trek among evangelicals and even Pentecostals to (Eastern) Orthodoxy. I decided I needed to get to know about Orthodoxy. I discovered that the Trinity stood at the center of the faith of the early church and it informed every aspect of their theological thinking. As a convinced Protestant, my theology classes became more Trinitarian focused.

But during this time I lived in a state of cognitive dissonance, not being able to integrate significant aspects of my Reformed/dispensational theological understanding with my newly developed Trinitarian perspective. About nine years ago I made the acquaintance of Baxter Kruger, who pointed me to the Reformed Scottish theologian Thomas Torrance. I learned from Torrance a theological perspective rooted in the early church understanding of God as a tri-personal dynamic unity, a theology that moved beyond the mere verbal affirmation of an abstract doctrine of a distant Trinity. I discovered instead the dynamic interpersonal relationship of the divine person(s) who love us and beckon to us to enter into the very *koinonia* that the Father, Son and Spirit experience with one another.

We all come to our faith with pre-existing God-concepts, or interpretive lenses, that we are not aware of but have a profound effect on who we understand God to be. These are unconsciously absorbed from our families, churches, and culture. I have endeavored to expose several of the popular concepts that warp our understanding of the reality of who God is. The purpose? To enable us to take off these lenses and look

13

at God through the lens of Jesus himself. As Jesus said, "Whoever has seen me has seen the Father (John 14:9)." Or as the apostle John stated, "The only-begotten God who is in the bosom of the Father he has exegeted (explained fully) Him (John 1:18)."[1]

Christian faith is not about affirmation of doctrinal propositions: it is about *life*, participating in *koinonia* of the Father, Son, and Spirit. This is the goal of the incarnation. He became one of us so that we might know him "up close and personal." The divine desire (of Father, Son and Spirit) is that we *know* him intimately and personally, not just know facts about him, not just be able to quote Scripture. While we can never comprehend him in his infinite fullness, the divine desire is that we participate in the dynamic fellowship of the Father, Son, and Spirit and in so doing be transformed into the likeness of the Son, our elder brother and the firstborn over all of creation.

I pray that this book might open up new horizons that will allow you to go, in the words of C. S. Lewis, "further up and further in." And in the words of Paul, "take hold of what is truly life."

---

1. My translations.

Chapter 1

The Trinity: Why Is It Important?

"... a riddle wrapped in a mystery inside an enigma."[1]
—*Winston Churchill*

Winston Churchill's observation about Soviet foreign policy is the same as that of most modern Christians about the most basic doctrine of the Christian faith: the Trinity.

When as twenty-first-century Western Christians we hear the word "God," what do we think of? Probably most of us think of a powerful, eternal spiritual being who is the creator of everything and the active agent behind the ongoing operation of the world. He is also, in most people's understanding, a moral judge who will ultimately decide who gets to spend eternity in heaven or hell as a just recompense for how we have lived our lives. He may send us good things as a reward for our behavior, or bring us trouble and even catastrophe if we do really heinous things. For example, we heard nationally prominent evangelical preachers declaring that the attacks of 9/11 were the judgment of God on America for turning away from him.

Astonishingly enough, as Christians we do not first think of God as Trinity, existing eternally in loving relationship as Father, Son, and Spirit. The existence of God as Trinity was the central affirmation of the ancient church and the truth from which all other theological understanding flowed. However, for us Western Christians (both Protestant

---

1. Winston Churchill, "The Russian Enigma," BBC Radio Broadcast, October 1, 1939.

and Catholic) the Trinity has faded into obscurity,[2] the light shed by its reality dimmed to the point of nearly flickering out. While we still verbally affirm the truth of the Trinity, for all practical purposes we have lost its meaning, and in the process have lost the biblical picture of Jesus Christ as Lord of creation as well. Were we to deny the Trinity altogether, it is doubtful much would change in our churches on a day-to-day basis.

Seeking practical "cash value" in our beliefs, and seeing no practical relevance for the doctrine of the Trinity, we have in large measure relegated it to the realm of "mystery." We can affirm it, but as one British theologian has stated, "The Trinity is the greatest mystery of the Christian faith. Therefore, leave it well enough alone."[3] Others say, "The Trinity: deny it and you will you lose your soul; try to understand it and you lose your mind."

These attitudes are the reason for this book. From a formal theological perspective we affirm the Trinity, but the practical reality is that we haven't got a clue why it matters. We may be told that God exists as Trinity, but this truth remains an abstraction—a concept that is never unpacked. Those who communicate this doctrine usually have no clue as to its importance themselves. The loss of the reality of the Trinitarian vision is a contributing factor in the fractured nature of contemporary Western Christianity. If we don't understand this fundamental reality about God, how can we relate to him in truth?

---

2. It is encouraging to see that on a scholarly level a resurgence of Trinitarian study has been taking place over the past three decades. While some of this resurgence reflects a genuine "sea change," with the Trinity being restored to the center of the lens of theological understanding, among evangelicals especially a significant amount of the newfound Trinitarian emphasis is still stuck in an Enlightenment paradigm that wants to found the doctrine on more "solid" rationalistic foundations because the historic affirmations in the ancient creeds are "outdated." The concern seems to be primarily apologetic, and misses the point so badly that it does not even hit the edge of the target. C. S. Lewis once observed: "I believe in Christianity as I believe that the sun has risen, not only because I see it, but because by it I see everything else" (C. S. Lewis, "Is Theology Poetry?" lecture delivered to the Oxford Socratic Club, November 6, 1944, in C. S. Lewis, *The Weight of Glory* [New York: HarperCollins, 2001], 139). Those who are trying to find more solid foundations are still looking only at the "sun" to try to explain it better or in a more contemporary manner, but not allowing themselves to see everything else in a profoundly new way.

3. Paul Louis Metzger, ed., *Trinitarian Soundings* (New York: T & T Clark, 2005), 5.

Over the next several chapters we will look first at some of the prevailing understandings of who God is in contemporary Western society. We then look back at the issue that first gave rise to Trinitarian understanding—the presence of Jesus on earth. This is developed in the subsequent chapters outlining early church attempts to articulate the relationship between the Father and the Son (and the Spirit). In the final two chapters we look at the way God has made and continues to make himself known in the world through the Son and the Spirit. Finally, we will conclude by drawing all this together into a whole.

Before we start our journey, however, I want to supply a little more background to the present situation. Karl Rahner, a Catholic theologian of the twentieth century, observed, "we must be willing to admit that, should the doctrine of the Trinity have to be dropped as false, the major part of religious literature could well remain virtually unchanged."[4] In a similar vein Catherine LaCugna states:

> If in the history of doctrinal development, Christian Theologies of God had adhered closely to the Trinitarian pattern of redemptive history, if all speculation about the nature of God were based explicitly on God's self-revelation in the economy of redemption, then there would be no difficulty seeing how a teaching about the mystery of the triune God would be germane to the various aspects of the Christian life. But for a number of historical and theological reasons leading up to the contemporary situation, *the doctrine of the Trinity for the most part has little bearing on other areas of theology.*[5]

While we Christians in the West continue to assert that God is Trinity, we in fact live our lives as believers in a unitarian God. If we turn our attention to the East, that is, to Eastern Orthodoxy, we find a far different story. In that tradition, God as Trinity stands at the heart of worship and theology. The centrality of the Trinity in Eastern Orthodoxy stands

---

4. Karl Rahner, *The Trinity* (New York: Crossroad, 2005), 9–10.
5. Catherine LaCugna, *God for Us: The Trinity and the Christian Life* (San Francisco: HarperCollins, 1991), 22. Italics added.

in stark contrast to its place in all versions of Western Christianity, both Catholic and Protestant.

The Western failure to apprehend and appropriate the truth of the Trinity has had disastrous consequences. These began to show themselves already during the medieval period with the re-adoption of Aristotelianism, but became more obvious in the era that inevitably issued from the failure of medievalism. It was during the Enlightenment (ca. 1650–1800) that the foundations of modern thought were laid. A crucial step in this process was the establishment of Isaac Newton's mechanistic concept of material reality, and this "clockwork" universe naturally led to an understanding of God as an impersonal monolith, distant and uninvolved in creation.[6]

It also led directly to a denial of the deity of Jesus Christ since the incarnation would involve a violation of the laws of nature—and God would never break his own laws! Newton, while a religious individual, was an Arian;[7] he could not in good conscience affirm the deity of Christ. Christian apologists over the following century gave a vigorous defense of the Trinity, but Newton's scientific explanation of the universe was both powerful and convincing. Within seventy-five years the intellectual descendants of those initial defenders of historic Christianity had themselves adopted an understanding of God's relationship to the world that was virtually indistinguishable from that of

---

6. The Enlightenment was a post-Renaissance philosophical movement (ca. 1650–1800) that denied the authority of God, the Bible, and the church (or churches) in the establishment of knowledge. Enlightenment thinkers asserted that true knowledge (including knowledge of God) is available to human beings via reason, and that revelation is both unnecessary and impossible. Deism, the rationalistic religion that grew out of Enlightenment thinking, holds that God created the universe as clockwork run by natural laws; while God exists, he is utterly transcendent and uninvolved in the day-to-day operations of the material creation. Morality is built into the structure of the universe and final judgment will be based on good works.

7. Arianism was a Christological heresy advanced in the early fourth century by Arius, then presbyter of Alexandria. In an effort to maintain absolute monotheism, Arius taught that the pre-incarnate Christ was a created being, the firstborn of all creation ("there was a time when the Son was not"). The Arian controversy led to the first Council of Nicaea in 325, which resulted in the condemnation of the Arian view in favor of that espoused by Alexander, bishop of Alexandria, and his disciple, Athanasius. M. James Sawyer, *The Survivor's Guide to Theology* (Grand Rapids: Zondervan, 2006), 547.

the deists—a clockwork image of the universe—although by virtue of a merely ad hoc modification of deism they continued to insist that God could indeed break in from the outside and perform miracles. In fact, early modern Christian apologists were themselves partly responsible for the origins of modern atheism by failing to employ the doctrine of the Trinity (specifically Jesus as the eternal Son of God who is co-equal with the Father) in their defense of the Christian faith.[8]

Enlightenment thinkers heaped scorn on the doctrine of the Trinity. Thomas Jefferson boldly declared:

> When we shall have done away with the incomprehensible jargon of the Trinitarian arithmetic, that three are one, and one is three; when we shall have knocked down the artificial scaffolding, reared to mask from view the very simple structure of Jesus; when, in short, we shall have unlearned everything which has been taught since his day, and got back to the pure and simple doctrines he inculcated, we shall then be truly and worthily his disciples.[9]

And forms of this version of Christianity have persisted into the present day.

The past three decades, however, have seen an awakening in patristics, the study of the early church fathers,[10] and this has in turn spurred a rapidly increasing focus on Trinitarian studies. This development of Trinitarian theology is not just another theological fad; nor is it simply a restatement of the doctrine of the Trinity in contemporary idiom, though there are some within evangelicalism who are pursuing this agenda for its own sake (and missing the point of the contribution of those in the forefront of the renaissance in Trinitarian understanding). Instead, Trinitarian theology is no less than a return to our theological roots and the basis of our faith. It involves *a commitment to*

---

8. See Michael J. Buckley, SJ, *At the Origins of Modern Atheism* (New Haven, CT: Yale University Press, 1983), 33; cited in Metzger, ed., *Trinitarian Soundings*, 7.

9. Thomas Jefferson, "Letter to Timothy Pickering, Esq.," in *The Writings of Thomas Jefferson*, ed. H. A. Washington, vol. 7 (Washington, DC: Taylor and Maury, 1954), 210.

10. That is, the leaders of the ancient church up to about 600.

make this foundational doctrine the lens through which all other doctrines are understood.

The term "theology" is derived from two Greek words: *theos* ("god") and *logos* ("word, discourse, line of argument"). The term itself implies that God, as he has revealed himself through Scripture and through nature, should be at the center of our theological reflection. Sadly, this is not the case. When someone first picks up a book of systematic theology, it can be overwhelming. The tome is comprehensive in terms of the sheer number and extent of concepts covered, but often without a readily discernible pattern to the contents: the book presents seemingly innumerable theological "facts" that seem to be related neither to one another nor to the spiritual life of the ordinary believer. The separate "doctrines" are often not tied together into "doctrine" (singular), a unified tapestry of truth that undergirds Christianity. Examining more systematic theologies a little more deeply, we discover that there is usually some kind of *externally imposed* unifying theme—but these themes vary from volume to volume depending on the theological tradition.[11] For Lutherans, everything is related to justification by faith; for Calvinists, the integration point is the glory and sovereignty of God; for those in the Arminian tradition human freedom has a central focus, while those in the Wesleyan tradition organize theology around holiness or sanctification.

Astonishingly, none of these traditions use theology proper, the doctrine of God as he has revealed himself to be—or more specifically Christology, the doctrine of God as he has revealed himself in the person of Jesus Christ—as the lens through which their theological understanding arises. This variety of theological starting points is a key factor in the wide divergence and even hostility between theological traditions. The new generation of Trinitarian understanding, however, insists that the reality of God as Trinity is *the* central truth of Christianity, and that as such it must be central to the task of properly understanding every aspect of the faith. In other words, every doctrine must be vitally related to the reality of the triune God. Taking this a step further will bring the person of Jesus Christ to the center of the lens because apart from

---

11. For a survey of the major theological traditions of the church, see Sawyer, *The Survivor's Guide to Theology*, chapters 8–16.

the historic person of Jesus Christ we have no entrance into the reality of God as he exists in himself.[12]

In this connection the late Colin Gunton observed:

> In considering the relation of Christology to Trinitarian theology, two distinct considerations must be held in mind. The first is that some account of the divinity of the historical Christ is a necessary condition of the Christian Trinity, as distinct from some merely rational triad. The second is that a firm hold on the material humanity of the incarnate son is a prerequisite for a doctrine of the Trinity that does not float off into abstraction from the concrete history of salvation.[13]

To unpack this a bit: apart from the historical person of Jesus, understood as fully divine in himself, the concept of the Trinity as we know it would never have been envisioned. Or if envisioned it would have remained in the speculative realm since such an understanding would not touch us directly in our experience of God. In pre-Christian Second Temple Judaism some of the rabbis did in fact engage in such speculation based on hints in the Old Testament text. But with the rise of Christianity this whole line of thinking was rejected and Judaism retreated into radical monotheism.[14]

If we were to survey the major religions of the world and put them on a continuum, we would find that at one end would be the religions of the East, which tend toward monism and focus on the unity of all things (the surface diversity is merely an illusion). Ultimately all is one, and that one is god. But this one, unified, all-encompassing being is impersonal. We find this underlying monistic vision in both Hinduism and Buddhism. At the other end of the continuum we find polytheism, which asserts that there are many gods. In the ancient world, particularly in the Near Eastern and Mediterranean world, the different cultures worshiped many deities. By and large

---

12. See Matthew 11:27. I discuss this further in chapter 3.

13. Colin Gunton, *The Promise of Trinitarian Theology* (New York: T & T Clark, 2003), 34.

14. This topic is examined more fully later in this chapter.

the ancient Near Eastern gods were nature deities: they had power over the various forces of nature. For example, in ancient Palestine Baal was the storm god, who was also regarded as the chief god of the Canaanite pantheon. Alongside Baal was his mother/mistress/consort, Asherah, the goddess of fertility. Additionally, there were innumerable minor deities associated with geographic areas. In Egypt, again we find a pantheon of gods worshiped as nature deities, such as the sun god Re, while other deities held sway over the patterns of life and death: Osiris was the god of the underworld and of the dead, Isis was the god of magic, and Throth was the god of wisdom. If we turn our attention to the Greco-Roman world we see the gods of Mount Olympus, on one level nature deities but at the same time human projections on a much larger canvas, bigger in both stature and power than we mortals while partaking of all the standard human passions and weaknesses.

On this continuum, then, we see in the East the all-encompassing deity of which everyone and everything are parts, a pantheism that is ultimately impersonal; in the West and in other areas of the world we see something more atomistic: a polytheism with gods covering every area of society and nature,[15] in conflict with one another and related to humanity in a master-slave relationship.

Turning our attention now from the ends of the continuum to the center, we find monotheism. The three monotheistic religions, Judaism, Islam, and Christianity, find a common root in the person of Abraham, ca. 2000 BC. But here we need to make a distinction. Common to all three is the reality that God is one, personal, and transcendent, but Christianity stands out as qualitatively different in insisting that while God is one, he exists in a plural unity of three eternal persons. This insistence that God is three-in-one and one-in-three leads Muslims[16] and Jews to suspect that Christians are in fact tritheists viewing the Father, Son, and Holy Spirit as three separate and co-equal Gods—a characterization that Christians absolutely reject.

---

15. I am for the sake of simplicity not addressing animism, that is, the belief that natural objects, natural phenomena, and the universe itself possess souls.

16. In fact, many Muslims understand that the Father, Mary, and Jesus are the three members of the Trinity.

The assertion that God is triune arises implicitly out of the New Testament and explicitly from our earliest extra-biblical literature. It would take the fathers of the church nearly four centuries to finally give a coherent and fully articulated explanation of the truth that the church had tacitly held since its inception. It is out of the Council of Nicaea in 325 that we get our initial explanation that focuses on the eternal unity and equality of the Father and the Son; nearly sixty years later, in 381, the Council of Constantinople reaffirmed the Nicene explanation and expanded it to address more fully the issue of the equality of the Holy Spirit with the Father and the Son. The Nicene (and Nicene-Constantinopolitan) Creed explains the nature of the unity of the godhead as triune in a way that is self-consistent and avoids the twin errors of tritheism and modalism (the notion that Father, Son, and Holy Spirit are not distinct persons but simply three ways in which the one undifferentiated God has revealed himself in history).

As we look at Scripture, we must acknowledge that clear references to the reality of the Trinity, that God is three persons in one, cannot be found explicitly in the Old Testament; it is a reality that emerges only as we encounter the person of Jesus in the pages of the Gospels and the epistles. And once we have done so, it is only in light of the New Testament that we see hints in the Old Testament that there is more to God than first meets the eye.

This raises the question, "Why would God present himself to humanity, and specifically to his covenant people Israel, for millennia as singular and only after two thousand years allow *us* a deeper glimpse into his tri-personal eternal being?"

I believe the answer is to be found by looking at the context of the world in the third, second, and first millennia BC. This was a world rife with idolatry, a world that believed creation itself was divine and eternal, not created—let alone created by a single God. It was a world thought to be inhabited by innumerable gods, each presiding over a circumscribed domain of the natural physical world and social processes, a world that sought to placate these gods and curry their favor by sacrifice. This was a world that thought the gods could be manipulated through sympathetic magic.[17] It was into this world that God spoke

---

17. That is, the notion that the gods could be controlled by rituals, spells, and rites

when he called Abraham. We must remember that when called by God, Abraham was a pagan from Ur of the Chaldees, a city-state in southern Mesopotamia devoted to the Sumerian moon god Nanna.

Polytheism was deeply rooted in all cultures of the ancient Near East. Clearly, from the time that he was called by YHWH to go to "the land that I will show you" (Gen. 12:1–3) Abraham was a worshiper of YHWH, but whether he was at this point a monotheist or a henotheist (worshiping one God, but recognizing the existence of others as well) is an open question. We find continuing evidence of polytheism throughout the succeeding generations of Abraham's family for more than one and a half millennia. For example, when Jacob fled from Laban's household, Rachel stole the household idols that belonged to her father Laban. During the four hundred years of captivity in Egypt there is again evidence that the descendants of Abraham were involved in some measure of idolatry. Likewise, even after having seen YHWH's power in delivering them from Pharaoh, and even as Moses was receiving the Law from YHWH, the Israelites immediately fell to worshiping the golden calf. And after Israel entered Canaan there were, over the centuries, nearly constant battles between covenant faithfulness to YHWH and the temptation to worship the Canaanite idols. Probably the greatest example of the "battle of the gods" is found in Elijah's confrontation with the prophets of Baal (1 Kings 18:16–40).

Over and over throughout the centuries Israel pursued other gods. The book of Hosea graphically portrays Israel's inclination toward idolatry as spiritual adultery. It is not until the time of the Babylonian captivity that the Jews finally get the message: God is one and holy, and there is no other god besides him. Idolatry was from that point on utterly rejected by the Jews. From that point on Judaism was and continues today to be radically monotheistic.

In New Testament times this radical monotheism was the operative mindset among Jews. Pagan emperors might consider themselves gods and be worshiped as gods by their people, but the Jews would have no

---

whose form imitated or evoked the effect they were designed to produce. For example, the fertility cults of Israel's pagan neighbors employed ritual cult prostitution to induce the gods to bring fertility to the land for another season: human intercourse would persuade the gods to have intercourse and so make the natural world fruitful. Voodoo is another form of sympathetic magic.

part of it. Their aversion to any notion of shared godhead with YHWH is seen graphically on numerous occasions, particularly in the Gospel of John. In the well-known passage where Jesus declares "before Abraham was I am" (John 8:58 KJV), he was perceived (rightly) by the Jews as making a claim to deity. Likewise, when Jesus referred to God as "my Father," the Jews understood it (again rightly) as an implicit claim to equality with God the Father. On both occasions Jesus' opponents picked up stones to kill him for his blasphemy.

Why did God not reveal himself as Trinity in the Old Testament? To the polytheistic mind, a reality as subtle and incomprehensible as the Trinity would simply have been lost, perceived as yet another un-remarkable instance of polytheism; it would have been assimilated as another clutch of gods, another pantheon like any other. God had to be understood as singular before he could be understood as tri-personal—three personal identities sharing a single essence.[18]

Having said this, on our side of the incarnation we can see in the very language used in the Old Testament (as well as in the imagery used there to describe appearances of the invisible God) an anticipation of the full revelation of the Trinity. The *Shema* of Israel is stated in Deuteronomy 6:4, "Hear, O Israel, The LORD our God, The LORD is one!" (NASB). While in our English translation this does not tell us much more than that God is one, the language of the Hebrew text is quite revealing. The declaration is: "YHWH [the personal name of the covenant-keeping God of Israel] our *Elohim* [the more general title for God that denotes power and transcendence], YHWH is one [*echad*, a word sometimes used to denote a compound unity]." While there are multiple Hebrew words translatable into English as "one," including *ya-chid* (which speaks of absolute solitariness and is, interestingly, never used to refer to God), the term *echad* does not necessarily refer to an un-differentiated unity. Genesis 1 says that "there was evening and morn-ing, *one* [*echad*] day": the one day was made up of two distinct parts. In other places the text says of the whole congregation that "they cried out with *one* [*echad*] voice" (e.g., Exod. 24:3). To give one more example,

---

18. Donald Fairbairn comes to a similar conclusion in *Life in the Trinity: An Introduction to Theology with the Help of the Church Fathers* (Downers Grove, IL: InterVarsity Press, 2009); see loc. 910, Kindle ed.

Genesis 2:24 says that "the two [man and woman] will become *one* [*echad*] flesh" (my translation). This certainly does not prove the Trinity in the Old Testament, but it is very telling that the word used to make the point of Israel's most basic theological affirmation allows for unity in diversity.

There is much material in the Old Testament revealing that God is not a monad or undifferentiated unity.[19] It is startling to read some of the Second Temple rabbinic writings concerning the person of God. Some of the rabbis reflected on the plural term for God, *Elohim*, and the term *echad*. They also pondered the "Let *us* make man" of Genesis 1, rejecting the idea that God was consulting with the heavenly court since no one but his wisdom was his counselor.[20] Likewise some focused on the enigmatic figure of the "angel of the LORD (YHWH)," noting that this figure is identified with the LORD (YHWH) in a way that is never applied to created beings. Some even went so far as to conclude that God was three individual hypostases (although they did not use that term) while remaining one;[21] in fact, it has been argued by some scholars that this was mainstream rabbinic understanding in first-century Palestinian Judaism. What caused the Jewish leadership to retreat into absolute monotheism was not so much the Christians' insistence

---

19. See Paul Blackham, "The Trinity in the Hebrew Scriptures," in *Trinitarian Soundings*, ed. Paul Louis Metzger (Edinburgh: T & T Clark, 2006), 35–47. Blackham argues from a number of perspectives that the doctrine of the Trinity is found in the Old Testament. The New Testament authors, especially the author of Hebrews, clearly present Trinitarian thought as embedded in the Old Testament. If the Jews were not thinking in these terms already, how would they ever have accepted this argument? The stumbling block was not, Blackham contends, plurality in the Godhead, but the notion that God would become incarnate. Blackham's argument has much to commend it, with the following qualification: while a careful reading of the Old Testament reveals the *concept* of the Trinity, it does not present us with a *doctrine* of the Trinity in the way Christian theologians understand the term—that is, not just as a recognition of the reality, but as a coherent articulation of that reality. This does not come until the Councils of Nicaea and Constantinople.

20. Many today say that the "us" here is to be understood as a plural of majesty, as when a king uses the plural to refer to himself. The explanation fails, however, because this practice did not arise until the late Renaissance period.

21. See C. W. H. Pauli, *The Great Mystery or How Can Three Be One?* (London: William Macintosh, 1863). Pauli, a Jewish convert to Christianity and later missionary to the Jews, wrote this work to demonstrate from the writings of the Jewish rabbis, beginning at the time of the Babylonian exile and continuing into the second century,

on the reality of God as Trinity as the particular insistence that the man Jesus was himself the Son of YHWH. By the second century any discussion of plurality in the godhead was reactively stamped out, and Judaism became, and remains to this day, radically monotheistic.

But even though the concept of triune plurality in the godhead was understood on some level, it was not an understanding that was anchored to salvation and hence to the incarnation of the eternal Son of the Father. This is the point that Colin Gunton makes in his statement quoted earlier.

When we compare John 1:1 with Genesis 1, we see that the apostle consciously frames his statements in the terminology of Genesis 1, giving the creating activity of God a Christological and Trinitarian framework. In Genesis 1 we read that "God said, 'Let there be . . .'" and so spoke the creation into being. John says that the agent of creation is the personal eternal Word who was face to face with God and is himself God. Similarly, in Genesis 1 we find that the Spirit of God hovered or brooded over the face of the waters. While the Jews generally thought of the Spirit of God as an impersonal force sent out from God, in the New Testament we find that the Spirit is in fact a personal agent who can communicate and be communicated to, be lied to, be grieved, and so forth.

---

that Judaism did not require absolute monotheism and that a triune concept of the Lord was subtly woven into the very fabric of the Hebrew Scriptures. Of particular interest is the striking parallel between the rabbinic understanding of *Memra* (Aramaic for "word") and what John says about the *Logos* in the first chapter of his Gospel. Alfred Edersheim in his classic work *The Life and Times of Jesus the Messiah* vol 1(New York: Longmans, Green, and Co., 1896), 47 references hundreds of verses from the *Targum Onkelos* (the official Eastern [i.e., Babylonian Aramaic] translation of the Torah) in which the term *Memra* is used of the presence of God himself. In other passages *Memra* is linked to wisdom. Pauli also lists numerous passages in the Targums and rabbinic writings where the Spirit of the Lord is hypostasized, or treated as an actual personal entity; for example, about the story in Ezekiel of the Valley of Dry Bones: "this quickening of the dry bones . . . spoken of by Ezekiel, is to be brought about by the quickening power of the Holy Spirit, *as a Substantive Being*, one of the Three exalted ones . . . in Him who is without end, because He had no beginning—God" (106). Pauli goes on to quote commentary by Rabbi Pinehas on this passage where Ezekiel addresses the Spirit: "'O Lord God, Thou knowest'; as if he did not believe that the Holy Spirit was able to give life to these dry bones." The point here is that Rabbi Pinehas viewed the Spirit as a substantive being as opposed to an abstraction.

When it comes to seeing the Trinity in the Old Testament, I believe the most we can say is that the language used there allows for God's further self-revelation as triune through the incarnation and Pentecost. As the Princeton theologian B. B. Warfield said almost a century ago:

> The Old Testament may be likened to a chamber richly furnished but dimly lighted; the introduction of light brings nothing into the chamber which was not in it before; but it brings out into clearer view much of what is in it but only dimly or even not at all perceived before. The mystery of the Trinity is not revealed in the Old Testament; but the mystery of the Trinity underlies the Old Testament revelation, and here and there almost comes into view. Thus the Old Testament revelation of God is not corrected by the fuller revelation which follows it, but only perfected, extended and enlarged.[22]

---

22. B. B. Warfield, *Biblical Doctrines* (Grand Rapids: Baker, 1981), 142.

Chapter 2

God and the Boxes He Is Put Into

God is spirit, and the people who worship him
must worship in spirit and truth. (John 4:24)

Jesus' statement to the Samaritan woman is unequivocal: God must
be worshiped in spirit and *in truth*. As Westerners we do not have the
issue with idols in the form of material images, ubiquitous in the ancient
world. When we worship, we worship in spirit, in that sense at least.
The question is, do we worship *in truth*? Several factors make it appear
that even those of us who are self-professing Christians, who claim to
worship God as he has revealed himself in the Bible, do not in fact
worship God in truth.

The American cultural understanding of God is addressed in the
recent book *America's Four Gods: What We Say about God—And What
That Says about Us*,[1] by Baylor University professors Paul Froese and
Christopher Bader. Their conclusion is that there are at least four dif-
ferent God-concepts at work even among those who call themselves
Christians:

1. an authoritative God who both judges and is closely engaged in
   the world
2. a benevolent God who is engaged but nonjudgmental

---

1. Paul Froese and Christopher Bader, *America's Four Gods: What We Say about
God—And What That Says about Us* (New York: Oxford University Press, 2011).

3. a critical God, judgmental but disengaged
4. a God who is neither engaged nor judgmental, who does not care in the least what humans do

From a Christian perspective, what is amazing is that all of these understandings view God as singular and unitary. It has long been recognized that American civil religion, which arose during the nineteenth century, is basically deistic. The American cultural deity is simply "God." He is the God against whose "acts" insurance companies refuse to insure. He is the one who looks out for our interests in public settings: the one invoked at the opening of the Indianapolis 500 to give good weather and a safe race. He is the deity invoked in the song "God Bless America." When this God is mentioned in a public setting, he is virtually never related either to the Trinity or, more specifically, to the historical person of Jesus Christ; in fact, the name of Jesus is studiously avoided. This ought to astonish us. However, we do not even think about it. Even as Christians we easily slip into a deistic mentality.

A number of years ago the science fiction film *Contact* (1997) caused a stir with its discussions about the importance of belief in God. The premise of the film is contact with alien life, and its central character is Elly Arroway, a brilliant young astrophysicist obsessed with the search for extraterrestrial life. She is a tough-minded young rationalist with no room for anything spiritual or metaphysical; any faith that she had in God died the night her father suffered a fatal heart attack when she was about nine years old. In the film she succeeds in finding extraterrestrial life ("ET")—or, to be more accurate, "ET" contacts Earth as Arroway listens and recognizes what is going on. What she hears confirms her wildest hope: we are not alone in the universe. This is the hinge on which the film turns. "ET" has found us and invited us to come and visit. The governments of the world take up the challenge, with the United States at the forefront of the project. A representative of Earth must be chosen, but who should it be? What criteria should determine the choice? The burning question becomes whether the representative of Earth should believe in God. Those in charge of the mission decide that it is critical to send someone who professes faith in God. But herein lies the problem: the word "God" is invoked without definition. Candidates are asked if they believe in God, but not what kind of a

God they believe in. The word "God" is a high-frequency one, but one emptied of content.

Lest you think this is just a plot device for a movie, leading New Testament scholar N. T. Wright tells of his experience filling the role of college chaplain when he was a young lecturer at Oxford University. As part of his duties he interviewed incoming students, a large percentage of whom informed him that he probably wouldn't be seeing much of them since they did not believe in God. Wright responded by asking them what God they didn't believe in. Almost universally, the God they described was the God of deism, distant and uninvolved, who would ultimately judge humanity and reward the good people with heaven and the evil ones with hell. "I don't believe in that God either," said Wright, and then proceeded to tell them that he believed instead in the God who had revealed himself in Jesus Christ.

While we may claim to truly worship God, the diversity of under-standings about God even among Christians argues that we do not worship *in truth*. We project and worship images that we call God, but which are in fact created out of our own brokenness. We simply do not apprehend God as he is in himself, or even as he has revealed himself to us. Instead, operating from our finite, fallen, and sinful understanding, we have inadequate concepts of God at best, and at worst patently untrue ones. As professing Christians, we may claim our conceptions of God are biblical, but in truth we *all* tend to create a deity by patching together selected pieces of biblical truth—with idolatrous results because these pieces fail to reflect fully or properly God's revealed triune nature. We do, to a lesser degree, what Irenaeus the second-century missionary bishop of Lyons accused the heretical Gnostic teachers of doing: the theological equivalent of taking apart a beautiful mosaic of the king, reassembling it in the likeness of a fox, and claiming that it was the same as the original because all the orig-inal pieces were still there.[2]

---

2. "Their manner of acting is just as if one, when a beautiful image of a king has been constructed by some skillful artist out of precious jewels, should then take this likeness of the man all to pieces, should rearrange the gems, and so fit them together as to make them into the form of a dog or of a fox, and even that but poorly executed; and should then maintain and declare that *this* was the beautiful image of the king which

Thus we create idols in our minds: mythological deities that we try to please, deities that reflect the brokenness and pain in our souls. At best our understanding of God is inadequate, but the distorted understanding we have has not been gained in a vacuum; it is colored by our personal history. Our own experience and woundedness tempt us to shrink or twist our concept of God. Our families of origin, people in authority who have sinned against us, and our own spiritual blindness all influence our God-concept. This in turn can have profound effects on our lives. Recent medical studies indicate that our God-concept can even affect our physical well-being.

Gail Ironson, a researcher and professor of psychology and psychiatry at the University of Miami, runs the Positive Survivors Research Center at the university. Her research is in the pathology of AIDS. She discovered a particularly interesting predictor of the progress of HIV in her patients: their view of the nature of God. Some believed in a punishing God, while others believed in a benevolent God. She observed:

> People who view God as judgmental have a CG4 (Helper T) cell decline more than twice the rate of those who don't see God as judgmental, and their viral load increases more than three times faster. For example, a precise statement affirmed by these patients is "God will judge me harshly one day." This one item is related to an increased likelihood that the patient will develop an opportunistic infection or die. These beliefs predict disease progression even more strongly than depression.[3]

Likewise, church teaching and experience, ideas from other Christians, religious art, and broader cultural factors including music and film play significant roles in defining our view of God. The film *Legion* (2009),

---

the skillful artist constructed, pointing to the jewels which had been admirably fitted together by the first artist to form the image of the king, but have been with bad effect transferred by the latter one to the shape of a dog, and by thus exhibiting the jewels, should deceive the ignorant who had no conception what a king's form was like, and persuade them that that miserable likeness of the fox was, in fact, the beautiful image of the king" (Irenaeus, *Against Heresies*, 1.8.1, in *The Ante-Nicene Fathers* [Garland, TX: Galaxie Software, 2000]).

3. Dawson Church, *The Genie in Your Genes* (Santa Rosa, CA: Energy Psychology, 2007), loc. 719, Kindle ed.

touted as "an apocalyptic horror flick of biblical proportions,"[4] portrays God as having lost his faith in humanity. He charges the angelic hosts to destroy the human race. At this I roll my eyes, shake my head, and say to myself, "Give me a break! Who thinks this stuff up?" But "this stuff" doesn't arise from nowhere. It plays off a popular apocalyptic mentality that made the *Left Behind* novels so wildly popular. It also taps into a common conception of God as the distant, holy, angry, merciless judge who is anxious to condemn.

Security and Understanding God

As finite human beings, we will always have an understanding of God that is *lacking*. Echoing the early church fathers, the late Scottish theologian Thomas Torrance observed that we can *apprehend* God, but we cannot *comprehend* him; that is, we can truly know something about him, but we can never grasp him fully as he is in himself. The hook here is that we need to look outside ourselves to see who he has shown and declared himself to be, as opposed to projecting on him our own ideas, feelings, intuitions, and wishes about who we think he should be. Our projections tell us only about ourselves, as the subtitle of *America's Four Gods* suggests: *What We Say about God—And What That Says about Us.* True knowledge of God must come from outside ourselves. For us to know God, he must make himself known to us. Christianity has always insisted that God has in fact made himself known—in the person of Jesus Christ (John 1:18). But we have treated this knowledge as information from which to construct theological fortresses to give us intellectual security and so to domesticate God, without acknowledging the spiritual and intellectual blinders that hamper our understanding.

Using the metaphor of the explorer and the fortress, evangelical theologian Michael Bauman addressed the problem of the boxes into which tight theological systems put us, and the disastrous results of this. While he focuses on the problem of irreconcilable paradox, his observations are directly applicable to the issue at hand—that is, the way we take a few pieces of evidence inherited from our family, church, or culture, or

---

4. Jacob Sahms, "Bravery of Angels and Men" (http://www.hollywoodjesus. com/DVDDetail.cfm/i/05A38D11-FF0A-D937-6071B9085D619768/ ia/87A1C240-08C0-F07C-9730A7BECFC69D1F).

discovered personally from Scripture, and then inflate them into a full-blown understanding of who God is. We end up with a self-contradictory vision of his person, simply ignoring Scripture passages or pieces of information that don't fit the system. As we begin our journey, his words are worth heeding. The following paragraphs summarize and quote his argument and imagery as they relate to the present discussion.

"You all know," said the Guide, "that security is mortals' greatest enemy."[5]

—C. S. LEWIS

Our perceptions of God are distorted. This is a given, due to the fact that we are fallen as well as finite. Although many deny it, not only our moral nature but even our cognitive processes are distorted because of the effects of sin. As theologians we select pieces of the truth of God as he has revealed himself—the pieces most acceptable to our fallen nature—and try to fit them together like pieces of a jigsaw puzzle. If some of the pieces seem contradictory or lead to a paradox, or don't fit in the mental picture we are constructing, we put them back in the box, saying something like, "The majority of the evidence leads us to this conclusion." Or, in making our own movie of the narrative of God and his interaction with people, we leave the irreconcilable parts of the truth we've been given on the proverbial "cutting-room floor," treating them as irrelevant waste material. In this I am not exaggerating; I have debated theologians and pastors who made this very argument. They have built their theological fortresses and hunker down inside. Surrounding settlements spring up under the protection of the fortress, while any who think differently are viewed as the enemy. The fortress—the theological system—becomes a point of security to be defended at all costs. Those who step outside its protection as learners or explorers, or even those who suspect it may have a hidden weakness and look for ways to improve it or its foundations, are ostracized. To put it bluntly, theological fortresses, while externally imposing, are often founded not on rock but on sand. Fortress theologians

---

5. C.S. Lewis, *The Pilgrim's Regress* (New York: Harper Collins, 2004), 204.

believe in the security of their fortresses. They see it as a failure of nerve to admit that the architects and builders have built the fortress from their own preconceptions and have consciously (or unconsciously) excluded pieces of material that have not fit their vision.

I can personally attest to the accuracy of Bauman's observations. I was recently confronted anew with this phenomenon while doing research on a major theological tradition that has its roots in the Reformation. Part of this research involved listening to a series of lectures on the tradition. The lecturer, a professor at a seminary dedicated to this theological tradition, held on to the construct at its center and was utterly and contemptuously dismissive of those members of the same community who attempted to nuance with other biblical and historical evidence some of the absolute conclusions in the received tradition. Instead of interacting with them so as to demonstrate any error, he simply labeled them "revisionists." It was one of the worst cases of the "I-know-what-I-believe-don't-confuse-me-with-the-facts" mentality I have seen in decades.

These individuals cling tightly to a particular interpretation of the Bible or, as in this case, to verses lifted out of their biblical contexts and strung together by logic. As Bauman observes:

> "Was it not the map of God—our Bibles—that led us here?" they ask. In one sense, of course, they are right. The Bible did in fact lead them this far. But not the Bible only. Their misreading of it is what led them into the valley of paradox. Their lack of strength and their insecurity led them to settle there and to build a fort. . . . [These] fortress theologians *interpret the intellectual security they have erected for themselves as the blessing of God.* The perceived blessing of God becomes to them the perceived will of God. "Hitherto the Lord has led us" becomes not only their reason for staying, but also for fighting. *They become the victims of a besieged mentality nurtured on autointoxication. Those who settle elsewhere or not at all are perceived to militate against the truth of God.* They must be stopped, the fortress dwellers believe. . . .
>
> I believe such *theological premature closure is due not only to the emotional weaknesses to which we theologians are subject as fallen people, but also to the systems of thought we adopt.* . . . I am wary of

systems. They are necessary for controlled navigation. . . . But *theological systems also tend not to accommodate the unexpected, the exceptional, and the untimely*—things that can be crucial to our continued theological progress. Fortress theologians are dangerous because they are trying to do the inadvisable, if not the impossible. *They are trying to reduce the multifarious complexities of God and his universe to the truncated confines of their own mental paradigm*, despite the fact that the world and its Architect resolutely resist that sort of reduction.

The surest sign that a theology is out of control occurs when that *theological system itself becomes the theological method, which is the hallmark of fortress theology. In such cases, that system usurps many prerogatives not rightly its own. That system not only colonizes biblical exegesis, it becomes its own measure of truth.* What does not fit cannot be fact. . . . Few theologians, if any, would either admit to the practice or endorse it. Most theologians, however, if not all, do it—me included. When we do so we fail. We must not allow our theology to be turned into a hermeneutic [i.e., a method of interpretation to be applied to everything]. We have things exactly backwards when we make external reality subject to our own particular brand of theology.[6]

A key problem we face in grasping the reality of who God is and what he is like is expressed in the Chinese proverb "Two-thirds of what we see is behind our eyes." Logic and rational thought will not give us the truth because our perceptions of reality are warped to begin with—and besides, we naturally tend to rationalize to serve the end we are already predisposed to seek as fallen creatures. Add to this the fact that the goal of God's self-revelation is not to give us information out of which to construct theological systems in any case. It is relationship with him.

The Truth beneath the Surface

Beneath the surface of a relationship with God lies the truth about what and who we believe God to be. What is God like? Does he really care? If

---

6. Michael C. Bauman, *Pilgrim Theology: Taking the Path of Theological Discovery* (Grand Rapids: Zondervan, 1992), 21–23. Italics added.

so, how would I know? Are the tragedies of my life (brought about by my own sin, the sin of others, and unrelated catastrophe) caused by him? We live day-to-day in fear, anxiety, and self-doubt, and through the lenses of these experiences we perceive God. This is not just a twenty-first-century phenomenon; it is as old as humanity. Looking carefully at the experience of Adam and Eve in the garden, we see the same dynamic at work. C. Baxter Kruger discusses the experience of our first parents:

The great disaster of Adam and Eve was not simply that they sinned or were disobedient to a divine rule. The disaster was that in believing the lie of the evil one, they became blind. And by "blind" I do not mean that they could not see physically; I mean that their perception of reality became skewed, so skewed that they could no longer perceive the real truth about God or about themselves. They hid from the Lord.

Why? Clearly they were afraid, but afraid of what? Of course, their hiding comes on the heels of their outright disobedience, and most people would assume that they were afraid of God's punishment. But then again, how could Adam and Eve stand *in the garden*, the recipients of such astonishing blessing and love, and be afraid *of the Lord*? Had God changed? Had the Lord who created Adam and Eve out of sheer grace and love, and poured such astounding blessing upon them, suddenly made an about-face? Had he ceased to love?

Surely Adam's disobedience did not alter the being of God. Or *perhaps it did*. Perhaps God did change, abruptly and radically— not in reality, of course, but in Adam's mind. As Papa says to Mackenzie [in the novel *The Shack*], "When all you can see is your pain, perhaps then you lose sight of me" (98). The belief in the lie about God's character swirled around with Adam's pain— the pain of his own unfaithfulness— and altered his inner vision, his perception of himself, of his world, and others. But most important, the way he saw God was altered. Adam projected his own brokenness onto God's face. He tarred the Father's face with the brush of his own angst. He took a paintbrush, dipped it into the cesspool of his own double-mindedness and guilt and shame, and painted an entirely new picture of a god with it. And it was this god, created by his own darkened imagination— not the Lord— that he feared, and from whom he hid.

The triune God did not change. How could human action of any kind change the being of God? Is the divine character so fickle, so unstable, as to be dependent upon us, or upon what we do or don't do? What changed in the relationship was not God, but Adam. He now projected his pain onto God, thereby creating an entirely mythological deity, a figment of his own baggage. But this figment was nevertheless frighteningly real *to Adam*.

Adam was scared to death. How could he not be? He believed himself to be standing guilty before a divine being who was as unstable as he. Sheer terror struck his soul. For in his fallen mind, he was staring down the gun barrel of utter rejection. In his mythology, he stood a hairsbreadth from abandonment and "the abyss of non-being." This is the problem of evil and sin. The impossible has happened: the truth about the love of the Lord is eclipsed, so eclipsed it has now become *inconceivable*. A profound blindness has taken over Adam's mind. He cannot see the Father's face. There is now a terrible incongruence between the being and character of God as Father, Son, and Spirit and the divine being Adam perceives and believes God to be. And for Adam, and indeed for all of us, the God of our imaginations is the only way God can be. Any other God is inconceivable.[7]

Our false concept of God, based on our own self-image and background, hides the true God from our view.

Decades ago in the 1950s, J. B. Phillips examined numerous examples of "too small" understandings of God in his now classic book *Your God*

---

7. C. Baxter Kruger, *The Shack Revisited: There Is More Going On Here Than You Ever Dared to Dream* (New York: Faith Works, 2012), 165–66.

Is Too Small.[8] In the following section we follow in Phillips's footsteps and survey just a handful of the major God-concepts we find among contemporary Americans, most of whom would consider themselves to be Christians. While each of these "boxes" latches on to a part of the truth, each one does so in inadequate ways that produce significant distortions in the biblical portrayal of God. Yet our understanding, whether adequate or not, becomes our security; we find comfort in the status quo because we know the rules. Stepping outside our comfort zone is threatening, even if the familiar is killing us—much like the phenomenon of battered wives who will not leave their abusive husbands because of fear of the unknown. Our theology, whether personal or arising from the tradition in which we have been raised, gives us a box into which we put God or, to use another metaphor, a lens through which we see him. It gives us a sense of security; we always know what we're looking at and who we're dealing with. Whether that security is a true or false security is another question. While we may live as if "what we don't know can't hurt us," that is manifestly untrue.

Boxes We Put God Into

Aladdin's Genie: God and the Prosperity Gospel

The story of Aladdin and the lamp is a medieval tale from the Arab culture that has come down to us in the *Arabian Nights*. In the story Aladdin, a poor, shiftless boy, comes into the possession of a magic lamp inhabited by a powerful genie (*djinn*). When Aladdin inadvertently rubs the lamp, the genie appears and explains that he is bound to obey the orders of his new master Aladdin, whatever they might be. As a result of the genie's magic Aladdin becomes rich and powerful, ultimately marrying the emperor's daughter. After defeating an attempt by a powerful sorcerer to usurp his power by stealing his wife and the lamp, the victorious Aladdin lives "happily ever after" with his lamp, genie, wife, and riches.

What does this tale have to do with God? From the perspective of the scholarly theologian, from the perspective of the Scriptures,

---

8. J. B. Phillips, *Your God Is Too Small* (New York: Macmillan, 1953). A nearly complete online version is available at Google Books.

and from the perspective of the historic faith: not much. But having said this, there is much prominent popular teaching about God that is strangely remininscent of Aladdin's genie. It is seen in the Health and Wealth movement, also called the Word-Faith movement or the Positive Confession movement. The movement teaches that through "faith" you can have whatever you desire. The late Kenneth Hagin supplied a three-step formula for achieving this:

Say it. "Positive or negative, it is up to the individual. According to what the individual says, that shall he receive."

Do it. "Your action defeats you or puts you over. According to your action, you receive or you are kept from receiving."

Receive it. We are to plug into the "powerhouse of heaven." "Faith is the plug, praise God! Just plug in."[9]

Kenneth Copeland, whose name is often uttered in the same breath as Hagin's, gives a similar list:

1. See or visualize whatever you need, whether physical or financial.
2. Stake your claim on Scripture.
3. Speak it into existence.[10]

Those in the movement see faith as a force that can be manipulated by our words so as to create what they insist the Scriptures promise: health, wealth, and prosperity. What is significant here is that we control God/Jesus by what we say: *"You create the presence of Jesus with your mouth. . . . He is bound by your lips and by your words . . . Remember that Christ is depending upon you and your spoken word to release His presence."*[11] While those who hold this view support it with numerous verses of

9. Gary Giley, "The Word-Faith Movement" (http://www.rapidnet.com/~jbeard/bdm/Psychology/char/more/w-f.htm); see also Hank Hanegraaff, *Christianity in Crisis* (Nashville: Thomas Nelson, 2009), 105.

10. See Hanegraaff, *Christianity in Crisis*, 109.

11. David Yonggi Cho, *The Fourth Dimension*, vol. 1 (Seoul: Seoul Logos, 1996), 83.

Scripture, these verses are taken out of their larger context and twisted to say something they were never intended to communicate.

Jesus does indeed clearly state that, through faith, mountains can be moved (Matt. 17:20; 21:21), and that our faith can bring about much more than we normally envision. On numerous occasions Jesus chided the disciples for their lack of faith, and the fact that we do not see more demonstrations of God's power would seem to indicate that we generally suffer from the same malady as the disciples. Faith by its very nature requires trust, boldness of action, and conviction that what is being attempted will be accomplished, as opposed to a timid passivity or resignation that lays concerns before the Lord with no confidence that he will accomplish what is requested. As the nineteenth-century missionary William Carey said, "Expect great things from God. Attempt great things for God."[12]

But the box into which we find the Word-Faith movement has put God generates numerous theological problems as well as the smell of *pagan "magic"*—seeking to control God for one's own benefit rather than growing in a relationship with him for who he is. Pursuing wealth for its own sake apart from a relationship with God is, according to the apostle Paul, idolatry (Col. 3:5).

God as the Kindly Grandfather

In the movie *Oh, God!* (1977) God is portrayed as a kindly grandfather who exists behind the big picture and is relevant for the afterlife, but who has nothing to do with the details of this life. Here God has no plan, and life is mostly luck and what you make of it. God is basically well-disposed toward people, but cannot be expected to intervene or do anything about what happens in this world; it is not his place to interfere. "It's up to you," he says. He looks on and hopes you will do well, and as long as you do your best and try to be happy he is content.

This box is common in American culture. Those who put God in it may or may not call themselves Christian; it is a box convenient for those who say that they "believe in God" but are not attracted to any

---

12. R. E. Hedland William Carey: Did You Know? Little-known or remarkable facts about William Carey, *Christian History* Issue 36 http://www.christianitytoday.com/history/issues/issue-36/william-carey-did-you-know.html

particular religion. We can observe several features about this concept of God:

- It is related to the deism that came out of the Enlightenment, but has been sweetened by popular romanticism.
- This God is moral and powerful (powerful, that is, as creator and judge, but limited in that he is excluded from the world) and human beings are his children by creation and for whom he wishes and hopes the best. He is kind but mostly uninvolved.
- This God knows nothing of Jesus as the eternal Son and incarnate Savior.
- This is the God of American folk religion.

From a slightly adjusted perspective we could call this box "God as Santa Claus." He is a god we look to when we need or want something, hoping that our prayers will be answered, but even if capable of miraculous intervention he may decide we do not qualify. Like Santa Claus, he knows if you are awake or asleep, he knows if you are naughty or nice, so you had better be good. And, like Santa Claus this is a God who rewards good behavior with good gifts, but will put coal in our stockings to teach us a lesson if we behave badly. He may even be somewhat capricious about handing out the goodies and coal, or his standards for doing so may be inscrutable.

To put a face on this conception of God we look at LaDonna. LaDonna grew up with a gentle and unassuming father from whom she learned to be considerate and compassionate toward other people. All her life she has lived out the value of service to others, starting with running errands for her neighbors when she was small. When she thought of God, she attributed a sort of foggy kindliness to him, but could not really conceive of him as a person. She served many underprivileged children through a benevolent organization in her state. Up until ten years ago, she thought of God as a kindly but distant being somewhere who didn't expect much from her except that she give to less fortunate souls with a free hand, in which case all would be well.

Then when she was in her fifties, cancer struck. Her battle with the disease has taken its toll on her belief that God would treat her as well as she has treated others. If you were to ask LaDonna today how she thinks about God, she would just give you a waggle of the hand that says he is not very involved in her affairs, if he even exists. She just isn't sure.

The Manipulator: God as the Cosmic Puppeteer

In the movie *The Truman Show* (1998), Truman Burbank is the unknowing central character in a worldwide top-rated television series. Unbeknownst to him, his every move is being watched by millions at all times. His hometown, Seahaven, is an unbelievably immense Hollywood sound stage. His friends and family and even his wife are actors in a carefully constructed fantasy. His life, his experience, his reality, rather than being free and spontaneous, is carefully scripted and manipulated by the director Christof, who does not particularly care about Truman but is entertained, along with an audience of millions, by observing his responses as a kind of artistic experiment. As the film begins, Truman is clueless about the true nature of his world. When asked in an interview why Truman has never guessed the truth about his life, Christof accurately and perhaps more than a little cynically answers, "We accept the reality of the world with which we are presented. It's as simple as that."

A series of events finally leads Truman to discover the truth. When near the end of the film Truman tries to escape Seahaven by boat, Christof orders a storm so severe that Truman's life is endangered. Christof is willing to see Truman drown rather than let him escape the carefully manufactured fantasy.

Some of us view God in a similar light, believing that he manipulates his creation in a similar way for his own purposes. The puppeteer box is most often found among people who adhere rigidly to an extreme form of scholastic[13] Calvinism, often called hyper-Calvinism,[14] which

---

13. Scholasticism is a method of philosophy and theology developed at the newly emergent European universities during the High Middle Ages (ca. 1000–1300). Scholasticism combined the philosophy of Aristotle with the teachings of Augustine. During the post-Reformation period both the Lutheran and Reformed traditions adopted the methodology of scholasticism as they constructed their systems of theology. This period is referred to as the era of Protestant scholasticism.

14. High Calvinism is "that school of supralapsarian Five-Point Calvinism which so stresses the sovereignty of God by overemphasizing the secret over the revealed will, and eternity over time, that it minimizes the responsibility of Man, notably with

developed after the death of the Geneva Reformer. Those who hold this concept of God believe that he has foreordained "whatsoever comes to pass"[15] in a way that allows creation no true freedom or contingency. The view has a certain kinship with fatalism, insofar as we are powerless to change anything, with the significant difference that fatalism is impersonal. The puppeteer God is personal, but a person of absolute power who relates to humans as objects rather than as persons. In this view, God is (like Christof for Truman) all-powerful, arbitrary, and essentially non-relational.

As this box is unpacked we find a perspective that in its extreme form interprets every event, even down to the smallest detail (what brand of toothpaste I use, which sock I put on first in the morning), as caused and controlled by God. Some who adopt this perspective even see God as the cause of evil. This was, for example, the conclusion of twentieth-century American Presbyterian theologian Gordon H. Clark who unequivocally contended, "God is the sole ultimate cause of everything."[16] He goes on to assert that while God is not the immediate cause of sin, he is "the ultimate cause of sin."[17] According to this understanding, human beings are objects to God rather than persons with whom to relate. As the cosmic puppeteer, God loves those whom he has chosen, but hates the rest of humanity.

---

respect to the denial of the word 'offer' in relation to the preaching of the Gospel of a finished and limited atonement, thus undermining the universal duty of sinners to believe savingly with assurance that the Lord Jesus Christ died for them." To state it in another way, hyper-Calvinism denies the "universal command to repent and believe" (http://en.wikipedia.org/wiki/Hyper-Calvinism, accessed April 25, 2013).

15. *Westminster Shorter Catechism*, question 8.

16. Gordon Clark, *Religion, Reason and Revelation* (Unicoi, TN: Trinity Foundation, 1995), 237–38.

17. Ibid., 239. In addressing this basic issue the Westminster Confession 5:4 states: "The almighty power, unsearchable wisdom, and infinite goodness of God so far manifest themselves in His providence, that it extendeth itself even to the first fall, and all other sins of angels and men; and that not by a bare permission, but such as hath joined with it a most wise and powerful bounding, and otherwise ordering and governing of them, in a manifold dispensation, to His own holy ends; yet so, as the sinfulness thereof proceedeth only from the creature, and not from God, who, being most holy and righteous, neither is, nor can be, the author or approver of sin." It would appear that the framers of the Westminster Confession recognize an inherent problem in their formulation of this question that they cannot ultimately answer and therefore attempt to define away.

One reason this box is popular in some quarters is that it can claim a lot of biblical support. There are many passages of Scripture that speak about divine sovereignty and divine election. When wrested out of a larger context and strung together, such passages appear on the surface to make a formidable case for this position. Moreover, this view is orthodox in affirming the core doctrines of the historical Christian faith, such as:

- God as Trinity
- Christ as the eternal and incarnate Son
- The sinfulness of all humanity
- The inability of human beings to save themselves
- The necessity of the atonement to bring reconciliation between God and humanity (i.e., those whom he has elected)[18]

It also appeals to our guilty self-knowledge by insisting on our depravity in contrast with the holiness of God. In its extreme form, however, it causes *God's love and the enjoyment of true relationship with him* to recede into the background. Instead, the demand on the believer is submission to God's perfect will as expressed in his decrees. This mentality slips into a sense of divine arbitrariness, inducing a fatalism among its adherents that in practice denies any genuine relationship or sonship with God. The attitudes exhibited by this form of Calvinism parallel those generated by the God-concept of Islam (which means "submission").

Cameron puts a face on this understanding of God. If ever you met Cameron, you would be likely to say, "Now there's someone in charge of his life." Cameron is a congenial middle-aged adult with two grown children. He has no reservations about sharing his faith in Christ with anyone and everyone. Looking a little deeper, you would see that Cameron's life is beset by misfortunes and struggles. The used grain combine that he purchased two years ago for the farm breaks down frequently, but he can't seem to move ahead enough to get rid of it and buy a more dependable one. He expresses his experience and frustrations about his circumstances thus:

---

18. It follows Augustine in asserting that the effects of the atonement objectively accomplish salvation of those whom God has elected in eternity past.

- "God is trying to teach me something."
- "I must be doing something that angers God."
- "If it were God's will, he would make sure the combine got fixed right."

Cameron's expressions of frustration about his life belie a combative relationship he thinks he has with a stern, overbearing, and controlling Father. It's much like the way he has learned to deal with his own unrelentingly critical and demanding earthly father.

The Wrathful God: Petty and Vengeful

Many see God in the role of angry judge. In the movie *Clash of the Titans* (1981) we see Zeus full of anger and vengeance,   which he directs toward King Acrisius of Argos. Acrisius has received a prophecy that his daughter Danae will give birth to a son who will kill him. To prevent this prophecy from coming true, he locks Danae up, away from all men. Despite Acrisius's efforts to protect his daughter, however, Zeus comes to her as a shower of gold and impregnates her. Learning that his daughter is pregnant, Acrisius commits her to the sea in a coffin. Enraged, Zeus orders that Danae and her unborn child Perseus be rescued and hidden. That accomplished, he strikes Acrisius dead by crushing an image of the king in his hand, and sends disaster on Argos as well.

Painting a portrait of an angry, bitter God has been and continues to be popular in film right up to the present day. As mentioned above, the film *Legion* is about a battle that ensues when God "loses faith in humankind" and decides to send his angels to bring on the Apocalypse to destroy humanity.

We may roll our eyes at such portrayals of God, but Darin Hufford in *The Misunderstood God* concludes that such ideas are not far beneath the surface of conservative Protestant consciousness. As a young pastor whose star was rising, Hufford sponsored a conference for Christian leaders, with shocking results. At the beginning of the conference he stood behind the curtains on the stage. Unnoticed, he gazed out at the crowd and saw a mixture of hope and disappointment in the eyes of the audience. Hope that the conference would give them answers to their questions and fears that had gone unanswered in previous conferences they had attended. As he scanned the crowd looking at the eyes he saw an overwhelming look of disappointment, a look he "personally recognized because [he] saw it in [his] own eyes every morning when [he] was standing in front of the mirror." It was a look of hopeless individuals who had been sold a bill of goods: a religion that didn't work. Rather than question the system, they had turned on themselves and entered a state of religious self-loathing that made each of them individually the problem, rather than question the system they had been taught.

Hufford determined not to let this be yet another confirmation of the attendees' deepest disillusionments. Stepping up to the podium he asked the audience to bow their heads and close their eyes. But instead of the expected prayer he asked a question: "How many of you are afraid of the Rapture?" Looking out over the auditorium he saw to his amazement and horror almost every hand in the building went up. This group was not a group of new believers but the heart of numerous vibrant active churches. He followed up his first question with a second, "How many of you feel you've basically been miserable for the largest part of your Christian life?" Everyone at the conference raised a hand. Hufford states, "The very thing I had suspected from childhood about the religion I'd grown up in was about to be confirmed." At this point he threw out the script for the rest of the session and they together "started down a path of total honesty."

Questions that had been for years demanding answers were voiced: the kind of questions that believers are afraid to ask because they sound pagan when voiced aloud. These questions were asked and addressed without condemnation. "We trod through all of those questions and came up with a conclusion that was both startling and simple. Maybe we weren't the first ones to discover this, but we may have been the first Christians to recognize it and not lose our faith because of it. Our conclusion that day was: We have been lied to about God. Who He is, what He is like, what He wants from us, and how He relates to us. How He responds to us, what He expects from us, His heart for us, His purpose for us, His desires."[19]

This view sees God as waiting for the smallest infraction of any commandment or law and using it as an excuse to cast us into eternal damnation; in fact, he may not even require an outright infraction in

---

19. Summarized and quoted from Darin Hufford, *The Misunderstood God* (Newberry Park, CA: Windblown Media, 2009), 5–7.

order to do so because he is basically disgusted by human beings in any case. In an episode of the TV crime series *NCIS*, investigators are being briefed about the depraved sexual crimes of two suspects. One of the investigators, who was raised Catholic, makes the comment, "I'm probably going to hell just hearing about this stuff!"

God as the Cosmic Killjoy (or Angry Policeman)

For some, God is the deity who kills all of their joy and punishes or puts a stop to all things pleasurable. In his well-loved book *Mere Christianity*, C. S. Lewis writes: "There is a story about a schoolboy who was asked what he thought God was like. He replied that, as far as he could make out, God was 'the sort of person who is always snooping round to see if anyone is enjoying himself and then trying to stop it.'"[20] According to this box:

- God is righteously angry at sin.
- God views pleasure as sinful.
- Salvation comes as a result of doing good works and not committing sin.

The concept of God as an angry judge or policeman, which arose during the medieval period, is still very much alive within both Catholicism and Protestantism. In non-Calvinistic forms of Protestantism, particularly among Arminians and Pentecostals, there is in the pews the common mentality that *each sin committed must be confessed in order to be forgiven*. In fact, if you should die without having confessed all your sins you are eternally lost. In these traditions there is a great stress on the necessity for moral perfection; some even say that every time a Christian sins, he or she must be saved again. I am not exaggerating; I have had numerous conversations over the years with individuals who subscribed to this belief. Likewise the former president of the seminary where I taught for almost twenty years related that, as a teenager, he walked the aisle to be saved again every Sunday night because he believed that he had lost his salvation during the week by sinning.

---

20. C. S. Lewis, *Mere Christianity* (New York: Macmillan, 1960), 55.

Recently I spoke at a pastors' conference of Roma (Gypsy) pastors in eastern Bulgaria. As the conference got under way I continually had to field questions about what I was saying. This went on for about forty-five minutes until I recognized the underlying issue and stopped. I asked these pastors (none of whom had had any formal theological or pastoral training) how many of them believed that they lost their salvation every time they sinned. While I was not surprised, I was utterly dismayed that more than three-quarters raised their hands. My focus for the day changed immediately; the topic became the unconditional love of God. These pastors, for all their sincere devotion to Christ, lived lives of slavery and misery; according to my host, the bishop of the denomination in Bulgaria, they were some of the most dour and miserable people in the world. They could not delight in life as a gift from God because they viewed as sin even the simplest pleasures that their non-Christian neighbors enjoyed.

Historically speaking, it was ultimately a reaction to this view of God that gave birth to the Protestant Reformation. As a young man Martin Luther had grown up with an understanding that the righteousness of God was that righteousness by which a holy God justly condemned sinners. As a sensitive man who felt the weight of his every wrongdoing and misstep, Luther tells us that he hated the righteousness of God because it was that righteousness that condemned him. He spent hours every day in the confessional, listing every sin he could remember and receiving absolution. But he became caught in a loop: the more he confessed, the more he remembered other sins he had not confessed. He cycled down into despair. He wanted salvation, but a salvation based on full confession was unattainable. His confessor grew so weary of hearing Luther's confessions that on one occasion he blurted out in frustration, "Look here, if you expect Christ to forgive you, come in with something to forgive—parricide, blasphemy, adultery—instead of all these peccadilloes"[21]

Inside this view is a preoccupation with not committing any sin because to do so offends a holy, just, and wrathful God. As with the cosmic puppeteer box, the formal theology of this box is historically

---

21. Roland H. Bainton, *Here I Stand: A Life of Martin Luther,* reprint ed. (Nashville: Abingdon Press, 2013), loc. 662, Kindle ed.

orthodox. There is much talk about holiness and pleasing God, but sin tends to be redefined in terms that make it more manageable. Some of the characteristics of this God-concept include the following:

- Sin tends to be an issue of acts (many having to do with cultural practices such as smoking, drinking, dancing, going to movies, etc.) rather than of the heart.
- Those in this box want an objective standard of do's and don'ts to live by.
- The result is a self-righteous and judgmental attitude toward those who transgress.
- Subscribers relate to God as slaves rather than as sons or children.

Macy gives us a picture of what this God-concept looks like in action. At nineteen years of age Macy loves hanging out with her friends, as long as there aren't any parents around. She thinks her father has the right idea about who God is, but also has experienced her dad as very stern and unforgiving. From the time she was about three, he has punished her with liberal whacks of his belt, even when it seemed she hadn't done anything serious enough to warrant spanking. She respects her father's intellectual brilliance, but no matter how hard she tries, she can't get close to him. On her part, she has kept many secrets from him, especially the abortion she underwent when she was sixteen. It gnaws at her. She has killed her child, and the guilt is unrelenting, sending her into whirlpools of depression and anxiety. The emotional distance from her parents is killing her, yet she knows that if she shares her troubles they would both come down on her with anger and judgment. She wishes she could be forgiven, but she is pretty sure that God is finished with her and has condemned her to hell.

God the Absent Father or Absentee Landlord

In the 1999 film *Dogma*, the lead female character Bethany struggles with the idea that God has a plan for her. Life has been unkind to her in recent years and she is surviving. She has a job and a home and faithfully attends church, but God has seemed distant and uninvolved in her life, indifferent to her and her struggles. Since she lost the ability to bear children and her husband left her, she has fallen into cynicism about God's love and care for her, and wonders why her original plan of marriage and children wasn't "good enough" for God. The following is a key conversation from the screenplay:

BARTLEBY
When do you think you lost your faith?

BETHANY
I remember the exact moment. I was on the phone with my mother, and she was trying to counsel me through what was happening to me and my marriage. And she said something like "There's always a plan." And I . . . just got so angry. I mean, I know she was talking about God, right? God had a plan. But I was like, "What about my plans?" You know? Like, don't they count for anything? I had planned to grow old with my husband and have a family; wasn't that plan good enough for God? Apparently not. How about you? When did you lose your faith?

BARTLEBY
Me? Years ago. One day, God just stopped listening. I kept talking, but I got the distinct impression that he wasn't listening anymore.

BETHANY
She. And how do you know she was listening in the first place?

BARTLEBY
(thinks) I guess I don't.

BETHANY
I hate thoughts like that. But they occur to you with age. When you're a kid, you never question the whole faith thing; God's

in heaven, and he's—she's always got her eye on you. I'd give anything to feel that way again.[22]

- This view of God as an absent father, like that of the doting grandfather, arises out of deism.
- In this view God is a provider who keeps things running but is uninvolved personally. He is beyond emotion.
- In this view God provides enough for his children to survive, but not necessarily to thrive.
- There is no vital personal connection between this God and us. He may not attend to our prayers or be moved to action by them.
- In this view *God's provision is substituted for relationship.*

When the Sherwins welcomed their baby boy Neal into the world, the crib was set up for him and the formula was ready to be prepared for the bottles. On the surface all looked good. But a closer look reveals little Neal alone in his crib with the bottle propped up. The Sherwins are hesitant to pick up their baby and hold him. Why? Somehow they never understood what to most people is common knowledge: infants need holding and cuddling in order to thrive.

As Neal grew, they kept their distance. As long as the baby was fed and changed, they were satisfied. As Neal developed, the Sherwins were careful to keep him under control and take him to church so he would turn out to be an upstanding citizen. Dad took that to mean that punishments should be meted out when necessary and that he shouldn't become too familiar with his son. The idea of hugging his child made him feel uneasy. It was best that he bring home the bacon for the family and then retreat to his armchair in the evening.

Neal is all grown up now and has a good work ethic. He rolls with the punches and appears to be okay. But a deeper look reveals isolation and loneliness. He accepts the reality that people and God can relate to him only by keeping him at arm's length.

---

22. Kevin Smith, *Dogma* (shooting script) (http://www.imsdb.com/scripts/Dogma.html).

The Lonely and Impotent God

In this box we find a somewhat romanticized view of God with some roots in liberal Protestant theology and prevalent in much of popular consciousness. It is a reaction to the indifferent, impersonal, almighty but uninvolved God of deism and Greek philosophy, but still assumes that God is a singular unity. This God is personal and by nature warm-hearted, but had no one to relate to. In his loneliness he created human beings in order to express his love, but now that everything has gone horribly wrong he is helpless to do anything about it. He is fundamentally good and loving, but is not very powerful. In short, he is more like a magnification of ourselves at our best, an elder brother rather than a father. He offers us his comforting spiritual presence, compassionate understanding, moral support, and superior wisdom, as well as the inspiration of numerous moral and spiritual guides and examples (including Jesus); he may even manage to do the occasional miracle. But he has no real solution to the problem of humankind.

All of our God-boxes obscure or downplay aspects of the reality of who God truly is.

The Dad Connection

We have looked at several God-boxes. Where do all of these notions come from? Psychologists have discovered that there is a consistent connection between our relationship with our parents, particularly our father, and the ability to develop a close relationship to God. We associate the term "father" with our experience of our male parent. When we are introduced to the idea that God is "heavenly Father," we project our relationship with our father onto our heavenly Father. If our relationship was warm, loving, and caring, we are more easily able to develop a close personal relationship with God as our heavenly Father. If our father was distant and emotionally detached, we will have difficulty cultivating a close personal relationship with God. I have a friend who has been in ministry for more than thirty years. His father was an abusive alcoholic who regularly beat him when he was in the fog of alcoholic rage.

Additionally, the only time he ever heard the words "I love you" from his father was when he was drunk. For him both the idea of God as father and the word "love" were poisoned.

If we grew up with a harsh and demanding dad, a capricious or abusive dad, an emotionally absent dad, a friendly but weak dad, or a passive and "hands-off" dad, *our dad experience affects our view of ourselves as well as the box into which we put God.* This is not to say that our concept of God cannot be modified. But that modification is for many a long and difficult process, while for others there is an epiphany of God's grace and love that can switch their perspective rapidly.

Billy Buchanan, front man for the band Fusebox, discovered this truth as he struggled through the reality of distinguishing between his dad (who was brutally abusive) and God, a loving Father:

> When Billy was 12, his family changed forever. "My dad was beating my mom one night," Billy says. "My brothers and I tried to jump in, but he threw us off."
>
> The vicious attack made them realize their dad might kill them. Late that night, the three brothers and their mom snuck away to live with Billy's grandparents. "It was like going from hell to heaven," he said. "It was safe. Those were peaceful days."
>
> Billy grew up, drifted from church, and became a musician. He spent his life partying.
>
> One day, he had an interesting conversation with one of the band's roadies. Billy asked him, "Dude, why don't you party?" His response was simply, "God doesn't like it." From that moment on, Billy couldn't get God out of his head. He asked friends questions about faith and God. And he began digging into the Bible. Finally, he dropped to his knees and said, "God, do something with me. I am a mess."
>
> Billy's life changed that day. He saw his heavenly Father in a whole new way. He saw that God loved and cared for him.
>
> And now, God has slowly changed Billy's view of his dad. He started praying for him and, over several years, he found his prayers and thoughts changing. "I used to be mad at him,

but now I feel sorry for him," Billy says. "God's put a love in my heart for my dad."[23]

"Growing Up Just Like Me"

Harry Chapin's now classic ballad "Cat's in the Cradle" tells the story of a man who lived his life as an absentee father, and the effects it had on his son. The song communicates a sad reality with profound spiritual implications. Unfortunately, we fathers tend to replicate our relationship with our father even when we try not to. One friend confided to me that he felt like he had raised himself because his father was so distant and unavailable. As an adult he and his wife adopted a lifestyle that kept his children close so they would not feel the abandonment that he felt, but because he had never been adequately parented as a child he had no model to work from. Much as he tried to change the model he had learned, he repeated the cycle. On the outside he was physically present as a father, but he was emotionally absent. He and his children are not close and they have struggled with their own relationship with God.

"I Am Not Who You Think I Am!"

In 2008 the novel *The Shack* was released. If you have heard of the novel or read it, you are likely aware of both the phenomenon and the controversy surrounding the book. As someone who is not prone to faddism, I ignored the book for several months. It wasn't until I was on faculty retreat at the seminary where I was teaching at the time, and heard several of my fellow faculty members raving about the book, that I decided I needed to pick it up and read it. By this time it was gaining traction and there was a tremendous amount of discussion both positive and negative.

Many, particularly those who could be legitimately labeled as "fortress theologians," have found the book unsettling, and not a few have labeled it as utter heresy. Others, such as Eugene Peterson, who is responsible for *The Message* translation of the Bible, have hailed it as a contemporary *Pilgrim's Progress*. Those who have made the loudest

---

23. *Campus Life*, "Ignite Your Faith: Is God Like My Dad?"_(http://www.christianitytoday.com/iyf/music/bandsartists/10.34.html).

complaints are those who have read it as a theology (which it is not) rather than a novel. William Paul Young, the author, insists that it is a spiritual allegory of his own wounding and healing; as such, it is necessary to remember that it is filled with imagery that is not to be taken literally. I read the book, and as I read it, I recognized the theology that was behind the story. It is the Trinitarian theology of the ancient church, a perspective that has been all but lost in the modern Western (both Protestant and Catholic) church: witness the cries of "Heresy!" leveled against the book and its author.

In the novel, the character Mackenzie (Mack) encounters God in a dilapidated shack located in the rugged mountains of rural Oregon where several years earlier his daughter was murdered. During every conversation his view of God—his God-concept—is blown apart by what he hears God say and how God appears to him.

At one point in the book God (the Father, who appears early in the book as a large African American woman called Papa) turns to Mack and says, "I'm not who you think I am." Although Mack realizes that God must be different from his preconceptions, that statement drives home an important point: although Mack thought he knew God, his understanding was woefully inadequate.

Instead of giving a theological answer to Mack's confusion Papa says, "Mackenzie, the Truth shall set you free and the Truth has a name; he's over in the wood-shop right now covered in sawdust. Everything is about him. And freedom is a process that happens inside a relationship with him." Mack, whose daughter Missy was murdered in the very cabin where they are standing, is still skeptical that Papa could understand his pain. Rather than answer she looks down at her wrists, which were scarred with the same scars Mack assumed that Jesus still bore. She answers his unspoken question.

"Don't ever think that what my son chose to do didn't cost us dearly. Love always leaves a significant mark," she stated softly and gently. "We were there together."

Mack was surprised. "At the cross? Now wait, I thought you left him—you know—'My God, my God, why hast thou forsaken me?'" It was a Scripture that had often haunted Mack in *The Great Sadness*.

"You misunderstand the mystery there. Regardless of what he felt at that moment, I never left him."

"How can you say that? You abandoned him just like you abandoned me!"

"Mackenzie, I never left him, and I have never left you."

"That makes no sense to me," he snapped.

She continues "Don't forget, the story didn't end in his sense of forsakenness. He found his way through it to put himself completely into my hands. Oh, what a moment that was!" Still wounded and confused Mack blurts out, "This can't possibly be true!" Papa responds, "I'm not who you think I am, Mackenzie." Her words weren't angry or defensive. Mack looked at her . . . and sighed. "I feel totally lost."[24]

As I said in the previous chapter, historically the Trinity is at the heart of all Christian understanding. But to us as Western Christians the Trinity has become abstract and virtually irrelevant, and has ceased to be a vital reality. In fact, none of the God-concepts we looked at in this chapter are Trinitarian in any significant way, although the people that subscribe to several of them are explicitly Christian in their formal faith affirmations. I would argue that the lack of an integrated and vital Trinitarian understanding of the nature and being of God produces an understanding that is at best a twisted caricature of who God has revealed himself to be in his fullness.

In the following chapters we look at the development of the doctrine of the Trinity and its implications. Particularly, we focus on Jesus and the Holy Spirit and their work in revealing who God really is.

---

24. Summarized and quoted from William Paul Young, *The Shack* (Newbury Park, CA: Windblown Media, 2007), 95–98.

Chapter 3

Jesus: The Way into the Trinity

All things have been handed over to me by my Father. No one knows the Son except the Father, and no one knows the Father except the Son and anyone to whom the Son decides to reveal him. (Matt. 11:27)
Conservative Protestant Christians, whose heritage is rooted in the Reformation that asserted the principle of *sola scriptura*,[1] look first to the Scriptures as God's inspired and truthful revelation: we know God from the Scriptures.

But this construct is challenged by Jesus himself in Matthew 11:27 (cf. Luke 10:22). What Jesus unambiguously asserts is that no one knows him except his Father and that God the Father is known only by Jesus himself. In other words, there is a *closed loop of knowing*. This statement is particularly astonishing given the context in which Jesus spoke it. He was speaking to orthodox Jews to whom had been entrusted the Torah! Jesus is unambiguously stating that even they, the chosen people of God, cannot know God the Father except through the person and by the will of Jesus. The clear implication is that we can know the Scriptures, even have them memorized and be able to quote long passages, but still not have knowledge of God. This was in fact the case

---

1. The slogan *sola scriptura* never meant what most Protestants today assume that Scripture is the only authority. Rather, it asserted that Scripture is the final authority. The commonly assumed definition has been more accurately described as *nuda scriptura* (bare Scripture). Such an understanding was absolutely rejected by the Reformers.

with the Pharisees, who prided themselves in their detailed knowledge of the Scriptures. Jesus chided them, "You study the Scriptures thoroughly because you think in them you possess eternal life, and it is these same Scriptures that testify about me, but you are not willing to come to me so that you may have life" (John 5:39–40). The Pharisees were experts in their knowledge of the Torah, but failed to grasp its meaning. It is possible, and unfortunately all too probable, that even while knowing Scripture we miss the point.

When speaking about knowledge of God, we must distinguish carefully between *knowing about God* and *knowing God*. To use the language of Martin Buber,[2] *knowing about God* treats God as an object; the relationship is an "I-it" relationship. *Knowing God* involves personal interaction, an "I-Thou" relationship.[3]

Returning to Jesus' statement in Matthew 11:27, we would be frustrated and in despair were it not for his final qualification: "and anyone to whom the Son decides to reveal him." We come to *know God* by divine, personal self-revelation, not by human inference, reason, and imagination. Simply knowing *facts about God* does not in and of itself constitute *knowing God*.

The Trinity in the Old Testament and Judaism

To return briefly to a key point made at the end of the previous chapter: the *Shema*, the creed of Israel found in Deuteronomy 6:4, states:

---

2. Martin Buber, an Israeli Jewish philosopher (1878–1965), stressed that actual relationship is at the heart of the mutual existence of two beings through *personal* encounter. This encounter is unstructured and non-cognitive (i.e., it communicates no information) but is nevertheless real. Buber used numerous examples of this encounter. The most applicable in our context is the non-cognitive mutual experience of two lovers. Buber proposed that this was the nature of a relationship with God.

3. While in contemporary English we use the term "you" instead of the archaic and to our ears formal, distant, and perhaps a bit numinous-feeling "thou," "thou" is actually a more intimate form of the pronoun "you." The knowledge that Jesus is speaking of in this passage is an intimate, personal, experiential knowledge of the Father—not just facts about God. We are of course not saying that God did not reveal himself in the Old Testament. Israel received the Torah and heard the prophets—but there was vast distance between the individual Israelite and God. God was not known intimately and personally to the average common Israelite—that had to wait until the incarnation, when God truly became one of us, and Pentecost, when believers began being baptized and indwelt by the Holy Spirit, through whom the triune God is present.

"Hear, O Israel, the LORD [YHWH] our God [*Elohim*] the LORD [YHWH] is one!"(NASB). Of particular significance here is the Hebrew term *echad*, translated "one." We saw that the term as typically used in Hebrew does not refer to an absolute undifferentiated unity.

Throughout its history Israel was tempted and frequently succumbed to idolatry, worshiping the pagan deities of the surrounding peoples or worshiping YHWH in an idolatrous way by treating him as one of those deities—as a manipulator and object of manipulation. It was only in the wake of the Babylonian captivity that Israel finally truly embraced the reality that there was only one God: YHWH, the personal covenant-keeping God of Israel. The Babylonian captivity drove into Israel's consciousness with a vengeance that YHWH was one, absolutely unique, holy, and transcendent. Israel's national consciousness from this point forward refused even to pronounce the personal name of God, always substituting the word for "Lord" in place of YHWH when the Scripture was read aloud. At this time, too, there arose a change in the concept of the oneness of YHWH: it was taught that he was an absolute undifferentiated unity (*yachid* as opposed to *echad*).[4]

But returning for a moment to God's self-revelation in the Old Testament, particularly with reference to the Trinity, I quote again B. B. Warfield's observation:

> The Old Testament may be likened to a chamber richly furnished but dimly lighted; the introduction of light brings nothing into the chamber which was not in it before; but it brings out into clearer view much of what is in it but only dimly or even not at all perceived before. The mystery of the Trinity is not revealed in the Old Testament; but the mystery of the Trinity underlies the Old Testament revelation, and here and there almost comes into view. Thus the Old

---

4. While the Jews still used *echad*, they came to interpret it with reference to YHWH in terms of absolute unity.

Testament revelation of God is not corrected by the fuller revelation which follows it, but only perfected, extended and enlarged.[5]

Or to put it another way: the Old Testament gives hints or clues that apart from further divine disclosure could not be put together in such a way as to conclude that in his oneness God was also three. There are intimations and pre-indications, but they remain ambiguous.[6]

Beginning with Second Temple Judaism (post–Babylonian exile Judaism), the personal being and nature of God in the Old Testament became a mystery, and it remains so to this day. Surprisingly if not shockingly, as God came to be understood in Jewish tradition, there was virtually no theological content. This trend began with the "sealing up of prophecy" (Dan. 12:4) and the recognized end to prophecy at the end of the Old Testament era. During the intertestamental period "God was worshiped in Judaism as the ineffable, unnamable One, and moral precepts and rabbinical interpretation of them took the place of theological content."[7] God came to be understood as the utterly incomprehensible, undifferentiated unity who could be *apprehended* only in his external relationship to the world and particularly in his interaction with Israel, but not as he is in himself. "For traditional Rabbinic Judaism the idea that the Lord God Almighty is open to human knowing in the inner relations of his transcendent being is just not entertainable."[8]

The New Testament: The Appearance of Jesus

When we grasp the first-century Jewish understanding of the person of God, we are in a better place to comprehend the religious establishment's reaction to Jesus and his proclamation. To say that the Jews were expecting the appearance of the Messiah is to express a truism. More to the point, in first-century Judaism there was no unified understanding of who the Messiah would be or what he would do. We might draw

---

5. B. B. Warfield, *Biblical Doctrines* (Grand Rapids: Baker, 1980), 142.

6. See Thomas Oden, *The Living God* (San Francisco: Harper & Row, 1987), 188–94.

7. Thomas F. Torrance, *The Mediation of Christ* (Colorado Springs, CO: Helmers and Howard, 1992), 120.

8. Ibid., 121.

an inadequate parallel to the 2008 presidential election in the United States. Then candidate Barack Obama campaigned on a platform of "hope and change." The U.S. populace was tired of seven years of war, tired of the anemic economic situation, tired of the political gridlock in Washington, DC. The electorate was ripe for the message of change, and viewed Senator Obama as a fresh-faced and articulate candidate who would bring the deeply divided country together and lead it in a new direction. The problem was that Obama never defined what he meant by change. People poured their own hopes into his rhetoric, so every interest group saw him as one who would enact their particular vision for change.

This is similar to what was going on in first-century Judaism: there was no unified expectation of what the Messiah was to be and do. Some expected him to be a religious reformer; others said he would be a political revolutionary who would throw off the shackles of Rome. These two major themes were further expressed in subgroups with different specific expectations. In fact, one group taught that there would be two Messiahs: a suffering Messiah and a Messiah who would deliver Israel politically. In short, there was no single unified expectation as to the identity and mission of the Messiah.

But the one thing no one anticipated was that he would be God incarnate. So when Jesus showed up healing and doing miracles and preaching the kingdom of God, he was understood to be a prophet. But the religious establishment, always suspicious of any threat to its secure place, reacted to him with hostility. In the opening miracle of the Gospel of Mark (2:1–12), Jesus throws down the gauntlet. The paralytic on his cot is lowered through the roof of the house; obviously, his friends have brought him there to be healed. When Jesus sees the young man, however, the words he utters have nothing to do with the paralytic's physical condition; rather, he says, "Son, your sins are forgiven." This can be taken as a deliberate provocation, a deliberate challenge to the status quo. The scribes who were there accused him of blasphemy: forgiveness of sins was the prerogative of God alone. They were right, of course; forgiveness is a divine prerogative. They were not open to the extremely strange and disconcerting possibility that this prophet, this rabbi, could be God incarnate.

Rather than look specifically at passages speaking of the divinity of Christ or of the Spirit, at this point we want to look beneath the surface and see how it is that strict monotheistic Jews could ever assert the deity of Christ—for that is, in truth, what the apostles as monotheistic Jews do in their writings.

As I have said, postexilic or Second Temple Judaism finally got the message that YHWH was utterly unique. He and he alone was God. The gods of the Gentiles were false gods, dumb idols. Meanwhile there was also an emerging monotheism in the pagan Hellenistic world, but its god was one that arose out of Platonic philosophy, a philosophy in which there was a strict dualism between the spiritual and the material: spirit was noble and superior, whereas matter was base and inferior, so that the ultimate goal for human beings was to become free of their bodies. This monotheism of Greek philosophy asserted that God, being utterly transcendent and wholly spiritual, could not have any contact with the material world. This god was devoid of any emotion since emotion was rooted in bodily existence; he was so transcendent, in fact, that he had no personality. This god was so utterly detached from the physical world that some of the Greek philosophers declared him (or it—a personal pronoun is misleading) to be even beyond being itself: an abstraction. His only interaction with the physical world was through intermediaries.[9]

First-century Judaism understood the nature of God's uniqueness to be expressed in two different ways:[10] first, he was creator of all; second, he was the continuing ruler of all. Unlike the god of pagan monotheistic Platonic philosophy, the God of Israel, although also utterly transcendent and unknowable as he was in himself, was personal. He was a God who spoke. He acted in history. He loved, yearned, became angry or jealous, felt pity. He could be personally addressed in prayer. He had a name: YHWH (though he is too holy for sinful humanity to pronounce

---

9. This is an aspect of Platonic philosophy that has made its way over the centuries into Western Christian understanding, particularly with reference to the nature of God's relationship to his creation. One of my professors in seminary, who was himself philosophically a Thomist (i.e., committed to the philosophical position of Thomas Aquinas) insisted that God could not touch the material order, so his presence was mediated by angels. I have never figured out how, operating from this presupposition, he could also assert the reality of the incarnation.

10. The following section summarizes the work of Richard Bauckham, *God Crucified* (Grand Rapids: Eerdmans, 1999).

it). And he was a God who was not arbitrary but acted consistently with his holy and faithful character.

While he is a God who himself acts directly in history, we also find in the Old Testament two aspects of the divine being that are apparently hypostatized, that is, treated not as abstract concepts but as entities having their own real existence: the Word of God and the Wisdom of God. Referencing Isaiah 40:13, the intertestamental book 2 Enoch 33:4 says that God had no adviser in his work of creation, but his Wisdom was his adviser. This means that God had no one but himself to advise him. It might be likened to us saying "me, myself, and I." The significance of such language is that the Word of God and the Wisdom of God are intrinsic to the divine identity even as they are recognizable as agents.

It is against this background that we must understand how the New Testament authors did not see monotheism as an obstacle in recognizing the deity of Jesus. The fact that the Word of God and the Wisdom of God participate in the creative work of God and in God's sovereignty while belonging intrinsically to God gives us the interpretive key allowing us to understand the way the New Testament texts relate Jesus to Jewish monotheism. Several New Testament scholars have called this approach "Christological monotheism."

Jesus Participates in the Unique Divine Sovereignty of YHWH

To unpack this a bit further we can look at Psalm 110:1. This verse is either quoted or referenced twenty-one times in the New Testament—more than any other Old Testament passage. It is the LORD's proclamation to "my Lord": "Sit down at my right hand until I make your enemies your footstool!" The apostles and other early Christians used this passage to assert something about Jesus that Second Temple Jewish literature refused to say about anyone: that Jesus participates in the unique divine sovereignty over all things.

This assertion is not made in merely a single passing New Testament reference; it is the centerpiece of the New Testament authors' explanation of Christ's divine identity. For example, the apostle Paul asserts that Jesus shares in God's exaltation above even angelic powers:

He raised him from the dead and seated him at his right hand in the heavenly realms far above every rule and authority and power and dominion and every name that is named, not only in this age but also in the one to come. And God *put all things under* Christ's *feet*, and he gave him to the church as head over all things. Now the church is his body, the fullness of him who fills all in all. (Eph. 1:20–23)

Likewise Paul asserts in Philippians 2:9 that as a result of his obedience the resurrected Christ has been exalted to a position that is pre-eminent over the entire creation. This is a position that involves worship, something properly rendered to God alone. We even find that the resurrected man Jesus is given *the* divine name (conceptually this must be related to YHWH, the personal name of the God of Israel).

> As a result God exalted him
> and gave him *the* name
>   that is above every name,
>   so that at the name of Jesus
> every knee will bow
>   —in heaven and on earth and under the earth—
> and every tongue confess
>   that Jesus Christ is Lord
>   to the glory of God the Father. (Phil. 2:9–11)

The epistle to the Hebrews expresses the same idea in chapter 1. Similarly, Revelation 5 portrays in apocalyptic imagery the universal worship of the Lamb who has been slain, while Matthew 28:17 reports the disciples' worship of the resurrected Jesus.

The Pre-existent Christ Participates in the Unique Divine Creative Activity

The apostle John picks up the other unique aspect of deity, that of creator, and applies it to Christ. His Gospel opens with a tour de force. In the first five verses he proclaims that the pre-existing Word, fully God himself, has existed in an intimate face-to-face relationship with God from "the beginning." Here John echoes the wording of the first verses of Genesis 1. In Genesis, God (*Elohim*) spoke and it was so. Here, the Word (*Logos*) created everything that has been created; John says emphatically that apart from the Word absolutely nothing was created. In these few verses John conceptually extends Genesis 1 into eternity past and says, in effect, that while Genesis 1 is true, it doesn't give the full picture. The "speaking" of God there in the opening words of Genesis is actually a divine person in addition to and existing face to face with *Elohim*/God. It is this second divine person who in turn is the agent of creation.

The apostle Paul picks up this same theme in Colossians 1: Jesus is the image of the invisible God.[11]

> He is the image of the invisible God,
> the firstborn over all creation,
> for all things in heaven and on earth were created by him—
>   all things, whether visible or invisible,
>   whether thrones or dominions,
>   whether principalities or powers—
> all things were created through him and for him. (Col. 1:15–16)

Similarly, in 1 Corinthians 8:6 the apostle asserts that the one Lord, Jesus Christ, is creator: the one "through whom are all things and through whom we live."

The epistle to the Hebrews is, if possible, even more emphatic: the author unequivocally states that the Son of God is the one through whom God created the world. Not only that, but it is also the Son who is the sustainer of creation—through the word of his power, or his powerful word. I would suggest here that the word is not merely a spoken word; it is, rather, the *Logos*, the eternal second person of the Trinity named by John in the first verses of his Gospel. This theme is picked up again in Hebrews 1:10–12:

> you founded the earth in the beginning, Lord,
> and the heavens are the works of your hands.

---

11. Recall John 14:9, where Jesus tells Philip that "whoever has seen me has seen the Father."

They will perish, but you continue. . . .
You are the same and your years will never run out.

The Road to Nicaea and the Emergence of the Doctrine of the Trinity

The New Testament authors demonstrate the conceptual error of Second Temple Judaism in its insistence that God was absolute unity. They do this by showing that Jesus partakes of the two key unique characteristics of Israel's God: creation and sovereignty. In so doing, the New Testament opens up our apprehension of God's self-revelation so widely as to allow us a glimpse into God's intra-Trinitarian being—into God as he exists in himself. Contrary to the understanding of Judaism and the pagan philosophers, we *can* know God—not exhaustively, of course, but nonetheless truly—as he is in himself.

But the New Testament does not present us with a fully developed understanding; it does not articulate a *doctrine* of the Trinity at all. It takes nearly three centuries for the believing community to develop more fully its Trinitarian understanding and hence a self-consistent portrait of who God is. I have written elsewhere about the difference between their vantage point in history and ours:

> During my first year as a professor, I was teaching on the doctrine of the Trinity. The point of my lecture was that our understanding of God as three *hypostases* (οὑποσασις, "person") who share a common *ousia* (οὐσια, "essence") had emerged out of more than two centuries of theological controversy and wrestling with the implications of the biblical material. At this point, one student's hand shot up. "What do you mean they didn't believe in the Trinity?" he demanded. "I open my Bible and see the Trinity everywhere!" And that is precisely my point. We who live on this side of the councils of Nicaea and Constantinople open the Bible and see the doctrine of the Trinity everywhere. But those who lived before those councils *did not have the categories that allowed them to see what we take for granted*. While the data from which the doctrine of the Trinity is constructed are found within Scripture, the formal doctrine itself is not an explicit teaching of the Bible, since it is not a

category of the Bible. It is a human construct that has stood
the test of time as a model that faithfully reflects, organizes,
and interprets the scriptural data in a coherent, self-consistent
manner.[12]

This is not to say that the church did not believe in the Trinity from
its earliest days. As we move into the post-apostolic era, we find that
the early fathers of the church are adamant. They assert unambiguously
that the Father is God, but also that Jesus is God and the Spirit is God.
We find in these early decades of the church's existence that the writers
simply assert the baptismal formula of Matthew 28:19. They do not try
to explain *how* God can be one and yet three, or three and yet one. It is
over the next two and a half centuries that we find several attempts to
explain the relationship between the Father and the Son in particular.

The road to the doctrine of the Trinity is marked by two and a half
centuries of theological battles. These battles generally focused on the
relationship of God (the Father) to the man Jesus Christ.

Docetism/Gnosticism

The earliest battles took place in the background of the New Testament
itself. We see this most clearly in the first epistle of John, where a major
battle is being fought for the true humanity of Jesus; hence the opening
chapter's insistence on the fact that the apostles have seen, heard, and
touched Jesus in the flesh. John is fighting against a group known to
historians as the Docetists, a group that saw Jesus as a spirit sent from
God, a spirit who took only the illusory *appearance* of physical form but
had no real human body. In denying Jesus' humanity they also denied
his death on the cross and his resurrection. John's answer to this heretical teaching was to declare as Antichrist anyone who denied that Jesus
had come in the flesh.

Docetism was grounded in Platonism, the worldview that saw spirit
as good and matter as evil—a presupposition common throughout the
Greco-Roman world during the first several centuries of the church's
life. Docetism has often been labeled proto-Gnosticism. Gnosticism

---

12. M. James Sawyer, *The Survivor's Guide to Theology* (Grand Rapids: Zondervan,
2006), 38.

can be described as a "New Age" movement of the second, third, and fourth centuries. It was not a single religion but a constellation of religious teachings sharing common presuppositions and expressed in several different varieties of spirituality. In the Christian versions of Gnostic teaching, as well as in Docetism, Jesus was a spiritual being who was sent from the utterly transcendent God, a God who could have no contact with the physical world. Jesus' mission was to teach a select few the special spiritual knowledge (*gnosis*) that would prepare them for spiritual ascent after death.

The Gnostics who followed in the footsteps of the Docetists also operated from a dualistic framework that saw nonphysical spiritual reality as good and the created material world as evil. While we have no intact writings of the Docetists, the Gnostics left us many "gospels" that portray Jesus in a fashion similar to that of the Docetists. In some of these Gnostic gospels, for example, we find Jesus described as leaving no footprints behind when he walked across the sand. In other words, despite an appearance of materiality he was purely spiritual. We might liken Jesus' appearance to a hologram that appears to be solid but cannot be felt: when one tries to touch it, the hand passes right through it.[13]

Irenaeus (d. ca. 202) wrote five volumes entitled *Against Heresies* in which he refuted Valentinian Gnosticism. Rather than attempt to disprove all the various Gnostic systems, Irenaeus believed that the basic presuppositions that all the systems shared were so similar that to refute one was to refute them all.

Ebionism

Another challenge to the full-orbed identity of Christ came from Judaism in the form of a group called the Ebionites. This was an early Jewish-Christian sect, whose name is thought to be derived from the Hebrew *habi,* meaning "poor"; the sect probably took its name from the scriptural admonitions to be poor in spirit (Matt. 5:3). They were akin to the Judaizers with whom Paul was forced to contend throughout his ministry. Originally the adherents of Ebionism were numerous—as

---

13. For a brief discussion of Gnosticism, see Douglas Groothuis, "Gnosticism and the Gnostic Jesus," Charlotte, Christian Research Network (www.equip.org/articles/the-gnostic-jesus).

numerous as those who asserted Jesus' full divinity. Many trace the beginnings of the sect to the church at Pella in the late first century following the fall of Jerusalem; from Palestine it spread to Cyprus, Asia Minor, and finally even Rome, with remnants of the sect continuing in existence until the late third century. While several varieties of Ebionism were manifest over that period and geographic area, they all shared common features: the view of Christianity as a new law, assertion of the continuing validity of the Mosaic Law, hostility toward Paul, veneration of Jerusalem, denial of the pre-existence of the *Logos*, a stress on the epistle of James, and ascetic practices.

While the early church rejected Ebionism outright, the theological core of Ebionite understanding—that Jesus was no more than a man—was resurrected in the nineteenth century by the theological liberalism that originated in Germany. Liberalism held that Jesus was just a man, but the only one who ever lived in unbroken fellowship with God. In addition, there has been a revival of full-blown Ebionite teaching by a tiny group of self-identifying contemporary Ebionites.

Monarchianism

The term monarchianism refers to the sole government of God, which is another way of saying that God is undifferentiated unity. Monarchianism was opposed to polytheism in all forms but also rejected any plurality within the godhead. Monarchianism came in two types.

Dynamic monarchianism (adoptionism) held that Jesus was a man who received special empowerment by the Spirit of God (understood as an impersonal force, *dunamis,* proceeding from God rather than as the third person of the godhead). Different teachers declared this special empowerment to have come either at Jesus' birth or at his baptism by John the Baptist. The man Jesus was thus understood to have been "adopted" into the "office" of Son of God, but "Son of God" was a title of honor rather than a denotation of inherent deity.

Modalistic monarchianism (modalism, Sabellianism) rejected the concept of three co-equal persons who were each fully God, insisting that this teaching was a form of tritheism. Instead, it taught that the Father, Son, and Spirit were successive historical revelations of the one undifferentiated God. God revealed himself in the Old Testament as Father-creator; in the form of Jesus in the Gospels he revealed himself as Son-redeemer; and beginning at Pentecost he revealed himself as Spirit-sanctifier. With reference to the Son, the modalists taught that while Jesus had a human body and was born of Mary, the divine mind replaced the human mind in him.

Tertullian (d. ca. 225), the first Latin father of the church, wrote the celebrated refutation of modalism, *Against Praxeas*. He called the heresy patripassionism (the Father suffered): "He [Praxeas] maintains that there is one only Lord, the Almighty Creator of the world, in order that out of this doctrine of the unity he may fabricate a heresy. He says that the Father Himself came down into the Virgin, was Himself born of her, Himself suffered, indeed was Himself Jesus Christ."[14]

In other words, modalism saw the Trinitarian persons as modes of being, mere temporary roles played in history by the one God. We could liken this to the different roles we all fill in our lives. I am a son, a husband, and a father—but I am one single person. Modalism (or Sabellianism, after its most famous advocate) ultimately cuts us off from any assurance of God's character as he is in himself since each manifestation is only a temporary role he plays.[15] While roundly rejected by the ancient church, this understanding was resurrected in the twentieth century by the United Pentecostal Church ("Jesus Only").

Arianism

Arianism (named for Arius, a popular early fourth-century presbyter in Alexandria, Egypt) was the most influential and politically charged controversy of the ancient church. The Arian controversy is fascinating theologically because it provides a stunning view into the relationship of pre-understanding (in terms of both worldview and biblical interpretation) to the definition of doctrine. Politically, Arianism provides an "up close and personal" view of power politics in the church as well as of the dangerous influence of secular political power on theological development. Ultimately the Arian controversy became so divisive and heated that Constantine, the first Christian emperor, called the Council of

---

14. Tertullian, "Against Praxeas" 1, in *Anti-Nicene Fathers*, vol. 3, ed. Alexander Roberts and James Donaldson (Grand Rapids: Eerdmans, 1976), 597.

15. For an excellent discussion of the pitfalls of modalism, see C. Fitzsimons Allison, *The Cruelty of Heresy* (Harrisburg, PA: Moorehouse, 1993), 75–79.

Nicaea to settle the debate and bring unity to the church. Space does not permit a detailed tracing of the Arian controversy, as interesting and enlightening as it is.[16] The purpose here is to focus on the theology of Arianism.

Arius was a Christian fully committed to a Platonic understanding of reality, particularly with reference to the nature of God: he was an absolute monotheist who insisted that the transcendent spiritual nature of the one God removed him from the possibility of touching the physical order. He maintained that the one God was, in himself, alone and unoriginate (i.e., without beginning). Not only was God unable by nature to become involved in the world, he was so transcendent that he could not even create the world; instead, the pre-incarnate Christ, the *Logos*, was created by God the "unoriginate" in order to be the creator of the material universe. Arius stated this position clearly in his dictum, "There was [a time] when the Son was not." He latched on to the term *monogenes* ("only-begotten"), used of Christ in John's Gospel (1:18; 3:16), to argue that the pre-incarnate Christ had a beginning.

> God Himself then, in His own nature, is ineffable by all men. Equal or like Himself He alone has none, or one in glory. And Ingenerate we call Him, because of Him who is generate by nature. We praise Him as without beginning because of Him who has a beginning. And adore Him as everlasting, because of Him who in time has come to be. The Unbegun made the Son a beginning of things originated; and advanced Him as a Son to Himself by adoption. He has nothing proper to God in proper subsistence. For He is not equal, no, nor one in essence with Him. . . .
>
> God was not always a Father; but there was [a time] when God was alone and was not yet Father; afterward He became a Father. The Son was not always; for since all things have come

---

16. We have dealt with this issue in a survey fashion in our book *Reinventing Jesus*, particularly in chapter 15 of J. Ed Komoszewski, M. James Sawyer, Daniel B. Wallace, *Reinventing Jesus* (Grand Rapids: Kregel, 2006). I have also dealt with the Nicene Council in a paper titled "Constantine, the first Christian Emperor," which is posted at the *Sacred Saga Ministries* website (http://www.sacredsaga.net/constantine-the-first-christia/).

into existence from nothing, and all things are creatures and have been made, so also the Logos of God himself came into existence from nothing and there was a time when he was not.[17]

In short, Arius contended that the Son/*Logos* was of a different substance and being (*heteroousia*) from the Father/God. Meanwhile Alexander, bishop of Alexandria, taught that the Son was of the same substance and being (*homoousios*) as the Father/God; using the same term as Arius, *monogenes* ("only-begotten"), Alexander and his protégé Athanasius argued that the Son had to be of the same substance and being as the Father since what is begotten of God must be God. A mild-tempered man who hated conflict, Alexander was ultimately forced to excommunicate his insubordinate presbyter Arius, who had gone so far as to accuse Alexander of the heresy of Sabellianism. As a result, Arius fled to Nicomedia (near modern-day Istanbul), where he was given protection by his old friend Bishop Eusebius of Nicomedia.[18] From Nicomedia Arius continued to spread his teaching, going so far as to compose songs embodying his heresy and teaching them to children. Soon his heretical doctrine was being sung all over the empire.

The church was in an uproar, split by Arius's doctrine. The emperor Constantine, a self-professed Christian though still unbaptized, desired unity in the church. When informed by his bishop that this was not an issue to be settled through negotiation, the emperor decided to call the first general council of the church to meet in the small resort town of Nicaea, across the Bosporus from Constantinople (modern-day Istanbul). The council convened on May 20, 325. Constantine had invited hundreds of bishops from all over the empire and paid for their transportation and accommodations; the number of bishops that attended is traditionally held to be 318, though some say the number of attendees may have been as few as 250.

The Arian doctrine was of recent origin, and a majority of the bishops did not fully grasp the issue at hand. They were still more afraid of

---

17. Arius, "Letter to Thalia," quoted by Athanasius (*De Synodis*, part II, chapter 15) in Philip Schaff, *The Post-Nicene Fathers*, vol. 4, electronic ed. (Garland, TX: Galaxie Software, 2000).

18. This was not the bishop Eusebius of Caesarea who wrote *Ecclesiastical History*.

the Sabellian[19] heresy than they were of Arianism. Consequently, as the council opened, a vast majority of the delegates held no strong opinion on the issue to be resolved. Arius was present, but because he was not a bishop, he was not permitted to speak. His position was represented by his friend and protector, Bishop Eusebius of Nicomedia.

Eusebius of Nicomedia "took the temperature" of the bishops in attendance and found no great support for Alexander's position. Evidently thinking in dialectical terms, he reasoned that "since they are not for Alexander's position they will support mine." This led him to expound the Arian doctrine in its most extreme form, stressing that the Father and the Son were of different substances (*heteroousia*) and that the Son was a created being who in turn created everything else. The bishops were scandalized; many covered their ears and cried out so they would not have to hear the heresy being espoused. According to some accounts Nikolaos of Myra[20] grabbed the document from which Eusebius was reading, threw it on the floor, and stomped on it.

The issue was put to a vote. The position of Arius and Eusebius of Nicomedia was declared to be heretical, and Arius and the Arian bishops were banished.

If you read *The Da Vinci Code* or saw the movie, you may remember the assertion that the deity of Christ was invented at the Council of Nicaea to buttress the position of the emperor, and that the vote to establish Jesus' deity was close. There is no historical reality at all behind this assertion. Christ's divinity was not at issue; all sides of the controversy held that Christ was in some sense divine. The point at issue was the nature of his pre-incarnate relationship to God the Father: was he eternal, of identical being and substance to the Father, or not? The divinity of Christ was already well-established from the first century on,

---

19. Sabellianism (or modalism), the belief that God is one undifferentiated unity who revealed himself successively as Father, Son, and Spirit, was condemned throughout the third century by numerous theologians (e.g., Tertullian) as well as by prominent bishops (e.g., Callistus I and Hippolytus, both of Rome). There was no early blanket condemnation because the church at the time operated as a system of "independent franchises" rather than having a unified hierarchical structure. The first official condemnation of any doctrine came in the Nicene Creed (325).

20. Nikolaos of Myra (270–343) was a bishop remembered for his great compassion and generosity around which legends sprang up. Through retelling and the accidents of history he is today popularly remembered as Santa Claus.

as is easily demonstrable by historical records; in fact, the early church was far more concerned with defending the true humanity of Christ than his deity. As for a close vote, out of the entire assembly of more than three hundred bishops, there were only two votes supporting the Arian position. Again, the Arians were not saying that Jesus was "just a man." He was still understood by them to be the creator who himself had become human, but in the *final analysis* he was only an exalted creature, a demigod, if you will, who was called "Son of God" as a title of honor rather than in recognition of his eternal divine being.

The issue now before the council was how to draft a creed that could be worded so as to condemn Arianism without allowing Sabellianism in the back door, so to speak. To this end the term *homoousios*, "of the same substance or being," became the key that locked the door on Arianism. Arianism stated that the Son was *heteroousios* (of a different substance) from the Father. The statement in the Nicene Creed that the Son is "of the same substance" (*homoousios*) as the Father was intended to exclude both Arianism and Sabellianism. However, for a majority of the bishops the term *homoousios* seemed to be either an explicit endorsement of Sabellianism or at the very least an open door allowing this rejected position to creep back in because the term had also been employed by a convicted heretic about fifty years earlier in a very different context. Because of this the majority of the bishops were hesitant about the position of Alexander (and Athanasius).

In fact, many of the bishops who voted to condemn Arius, Eusebius of Nicomedia, and their supporters had serious qualms about the term *homoousios* as it was used in the creed, but since the emperor himself supported the terminology on the advice of his bishop, they went along with it. In other words, the wording of the creed was a politically enforced decision that did not have the wholehearted support of the bishops. This lack of wholehearted support for the creed by a majority who still did not understand the full theological ramifications of Arianism provided a wedge for the Arians to cause division among their opponents and creep back in.

The following fifty-six years witnessed fierce theological warfare between the Arians and the supporters of Nicaea. By this time Athanasius had become bishop of Alexandria and the indefatigable defender of the Nicene definition. Finally, at the Council of Constantinople in 381, the

misunderstandings were worked out between those who wholehearted-
ly supported the Nicene Creed and the non-Arians who still had qualms
about it. The content of the Nicene Creed was affirmed and Arianism
was finally condemned.

The Nicene Creed (325)

We believe in one God, the Father, All Governing,
Creator of all things visible and invisible;
And in one Lord JESUS CHRIST, the Son of God, begotten
of the Father [the only-begotten; that is, of the essence of the
Father, God of God], Light of Light, very God of very God,
begotten, not made, being of one substance (όμοούσιον) with
the Father; by whom all things were made [both in heaven
and on earth]; who for us men, and for our salvation, came
down and was incarnate and was made man; he suffered, and
the third day he rose again, ascended into heaven; from thence
he shall come to judge the quick and the dead;
And in the Holy Spirit.
[But those who say: 'There was a time when he was not;' and
'He was not before he was made;' and 'He was made out of
nothing,' or 'He is of another substance' or 'essence,' or 'The
Son of God is created,' or 'changeable,' or 'alterable'—they are
condemned by the holy catholic and apostolic church.][21]

---

21. This translation of the creed is given by Philip Schaff, *Creeds of Christendom*,
vol. 1, 29 (http://www.ccel.org/ccel/schaff/creeds1.iv.iii.html, 2013) (originally
published by Harper & Bros., 1877). The bracketed material is not generally included
in later reproductions of the text, although it was in the original creed.

Chapter 4

God, Three-in-One

How are we to understand God properly? As Papa says in *The Shack*, "I'm not who you think I am." Beginning with the Council of Nicaea the early church unequivocally affirmed that God must be understood from a Trinitarian perspective. But what does that mean?

Over the past several years I have been heavily involved in studying and reflecting anew on the person of God. I became convinced more than twenty years ago that our Western understanding of the Trinity had departed from that articulated by the early church at the councils of Nicaea and Constantinople as well as the explanation given by Athanasius and Cyril of Alexandria, Hilary of Poitiers, and, to a lesser extent, the three Cappadocian theologians: Basil the Great, Gregory of Nyssa, and Gregory of Nazianzus.[1]

It was they who unpacked the implications of the pre-incarnate Son being *homoousios* (of the same substance and being) with the Father. Contrary to the Greek concept of the one god as a passionless, detached, "unmoved mover," the triune God who revealed himself to humanity, entered the world, and stood at the center of the faith embraced by the early church fathers was three persons, Father, Son, and Spirit, in a dynamic relationship of love. Some of the fathers spoke of this relationship

---

1. One of the most complete examinations of the Trinity from a historical perspective is Thomas F. Torrance's magisterial work, *The Trinitarian Faith: The Evangelical Theology of the Ancient Catholic Faith* (Edinburgh: T & T Clark, 2000).

as a magnificent divine dance. God is fundamentally tri-personal, existing in self-giving love. As the apostle John unequivocally states, "God is love" (1 John 4:8). And while it may be self-evident, it bears saying that *love, by definition, demands relationship*. If God was a solitary monad before creating, then he is not love by nature.

In this chapter we take a more in-depth look at the Christian understanding of God as Trinity and some of the implications of this reality. It is this Trinitarian conception of God that sets Christianity apart from all other religions of the world. As noted in chapter 1, historically the religions of the world tend in one of two directions, polytheism or monism. While radical polytheism is no longer a major issue given the way so-called pagan religion articulates itself today, "oneness" remains an issue because of its ambiguity. On the one hand, some insist that God is indivisible, is absolutely and simply one. In these religions the eternal God is utterly transcendent and removed from the created temporal order, so far removed that he cannot come in contact with it in any real way. On the other hand, there is an emphasis on another type of unity: the unity and connectedness of all existence. This is the direction that Eastern religions such as Hinduism and Buddhism have taken. It leads directly to pantheism (everything is god), where all is interconnected and divine, but ultimately all individuality and personhood is lost.

We see an insistence on oneness and transcendence in Judaism. Its central theological affirmation is the *Shema*, which says, "Hear, O Israel, YHWH [the LORD, the personal covenant-keeping God of Israel] our *Elohim* [the name of God that stressed his transcendent universal majesty], YHWH is one" (Deut. 6:4). Likewise, among the Muslims, we find the creed "There is no God but Allah, and Muhammad is his Messenger." But in both Judaism and Islam God is distant and unapproachable—or, to put it colloquially, the one transcendent God does not have a face. That does not mean he is not thought of as loving, merciful, or faithful, capable of emotions such as anger or indignation, and interested in human affairs; but he is unknowable and not intimately related to human beings.

When we recall Paul's experience in Athens (Acts 17) we think of rampant polytheism; it is said of ancient Athens in the time of Paul that it was easier to find a god there than a man. However, the situation in the Roman Empire changed radically during the next two and a half centuries. Under the influence of Platonic, Middle Platonic, and Neoplatonic philosophy, monotheism was no longer the purview of Jews and Christians alone; prominent articulations of non-Christian and non-Jewish religion were increasingly monotheistic, in a phenomenon generally referred to as "pagan monotheism." When it came to the various pagan deities identified with natural phenomena, pagan monotheists regarded them philosophically as merely mythologized images of one remote, impersonal, and unknowable deity, or they worshiped one of them exclusively as the greatest. The emperor Constantius Chlorus, father of Constantine the Great, was a pagan monotheist who worshiped *Sol Invictus*, the unconquered Sun.

Christianity arose out of Jewish monotheism and took root in the Mediterranean basin, within a (philosophical) worldview that stressed the utter transcendence of god and the transitory nature of all that was material. This philosophical god was the god of Plato and Aristotle and other prominent Greek philosophers. This god was the first cause, singular and indivisible, the unmoved mover; powerful, remote, and impersonal, unconcerned with all lesser beings. Within this worldview many religions, such as the mystery religions and later the Gnostic religions, sought to escape the material world and be united with this god in a purely spiritual existence. The Athenians scoffed, therefore, at the message of the resurrection when the apostle Paul proclaimed the risen Jesus on the Areopagus; the Greek hope, after all, was to escape the body—the prison of the soul—and be freed from the fetters of material existence.

As Christianity took root, therefore, it was at odds with both monotheistic Judaism and pagan philosophy. The apostle John, a monotheistic Jew, opens his Gospel with an emphatic statement of plurality within God, a plurality characterized by intimate face-to-face relationship. As noted earlier, the apostle intentionally patterns the opening verses of his Gospel after the introductory verses of Genesis, fleshing out the content of the latter by identifying the creator as the one who has become flesh in the person of Jesus the Messiah.

The pronouncement of Nicaea is both monumental and astonishing. It is the only creedal pronouncement of the church accepted by every branch of Christianity that has developed since that time.[2] In particular, however, the Orthodox Church (Greek, Russian, Syrian, and other branches of Orthodoxy) has made the Trinity, and the person of Christ in the context of the Trinity, central in its theological understanding. I recently had lunch with a pastor who recounted his visit to an Orthodox church. He was particularly impressed that during the tour of the church the priest took great pains to explain both the Trinity and how the Trinity was related to the person of Christ. Even the artwork and the icons of the church pointed to or were designed as a visual illustration of the mystery of the Trinity.

This centrality of the Trinity in Orthodoxy stands in stark contrast to its place in all versions of Western Christianity, both Catholic and Protestant. While we in the West continue to confess verbally that God is Trinity, many of us in fact live our Christian lives as mere "monotheists." As Catholic theologian Karl Rahner observed, "we must be willing to admit that, should the doctrine of the Trinity have to be dropped as false, the major part of religious literature could well remain virtually unchanged."[3] Even in speaking of the incarnation, that "God" became man, we lose sight of the fact that it was the second person of the Trinity, specifically the *Logos*, who was incarnated. While our formal theology may say that it was the second person of the Trinity who became man, in our minds and hearts the concept of the incarnation would remain even without the Trinity behind it. "For God would still as (the one) person, have become man, which is in fact about all the average Christian explicitly grasps when he confesses the incarnation."[4]

To put it another way, we live as practical modalists/Sabellians. We speak of God generically without reflecting on the three persons that we assert in our creeds or doctrinal statements or in the hymns we sing. When explained, the Trinity is described abstractly without reference

---

2. I do not mean that every denomination or individual church has endorsed Nicaea. Among Protestants, Liberal theology has rejected the Trinity. Likewise during the Reformation the Socinians saw God as simply one. In denying the Trinity, both groups denied the deity of Christ, seeing him as just a man. Another contemporary group that denies the Trinity is the United Pentecostal Church. This denomination has embraced the ancient heresy of Sabellius, asserting that "Jesus only" is God.

3. Karl Rahner, *The Trinity* (New York: Crossroad, 2005), 9–10.

4. Ibid., 11.

to the distinctness of the divine *hypostases* (i.e., the three persons of the godhead who together constitute the Trinity). To understand the *significance* of the individual members of the Trinity as persons/hypostases is virtually never even attempted.

Since the time of Augustine (d. 430) and the Western church's departure from the earlier patristic understanding, it has been common teaching among theologians that any one of the three persons of the Trinity could have become incarnate. In other words, the fact that it was the *Logos* who became man was a free and arbitrary decision among the members of the Trinity. The result is "that the incarnation of precisely this person can tell us nothing about the peculiar features of this personality within the divinity."[5] Rahner is correct here. And as a theologian I must confess that, earlier in my career, I taught for years that any one of the persons of the Trinity could have become incarnate. It was only in recent years as I began studying the foundations of Trinitarian understanding, getting beneath the surface of the "bumper sticker" slogans about the Trinity and wrestling with the way the Trinity was conceived particularly by Athanasius and his contemporaries, that I recognized how fundamentally wrong-headed the Trinitarian conceptions were that I had absorbed over the decades.

In college and again in seminary I took courses in the doctrine of God (theology proper). These courses examined in-depth the issues of the existence and attributes of God. They also delved into the philosophical proofs for God's existence as formulated by Thomas Aquinas, Anselm of Canterbury, and others. I learned how to classify the divine attributes as communicable (those common to both God and humanity) and incommunicable (those that characterize God alone).

The first definition of God that I learned as a junior in college was "God is spirit, infinite, and holy." I later became familiar with the Westminster Confession and the *Larger* and *Smaller Catechisms'* definition of God. More than a slight expansion of the above definition, question 7 of the *Larger Catechism* is as follows:

---

5. Ibid. Rahner goes on to say, "There is something strange here. Every doctrine of the Trinity must emphasize that the 'hypostasis' is precisely that in God through which Father, Son, and Spirit are distinct from one another; that, wherever there exists between them a real, univocal correspondence, there is absolute numerical identity."

Question: What is God?

Answer: God is a Spirit, in and of himself infinite in being, glory, blessedness, and perfection; all-sufficient, eternal, unchangeable, incomprehensible, everywhere present, almighty, knowing all things, most wise, most holy, most just, most merciful and gracious, long-suffering, and abundant in goodness and truth.

That in itself is quite a mouthful (though the Westminster Confession's definition is even more comprehensive), and it is biblical. Numerous Bible verses are cited as proofs of the truth of each part of the statement. But does it get to the point?

Actually, although it is thoroughly biblical insofar as it cites Scripture for every assertion it makes, I believe it misses the point by phrasing its first question about God in terms of "what" rather than "who." Additionally, it is significant that neither the Confession nor the catechisms even mention the ringing affirmation of the apostle John in both his Gospel and his first epistle: God is love! In defining God, the Westminster divines treated God as an "it" as opposed to a "thou": an object, a thing, as opposed to a person. Throughout the Confession and the catechisms the tone is clinical and impersonal. I find it striking that both Jews and Muslims could agree with the Westminster Confession and catechisms' definition of God.

As I did my doctoral work in historical theology I discovered that the preoccupation of the ancient church was not the existence and attributes of God, or proofs for God's existence. The early church was focused on the Trinity—a topic barely covered in my courses on the doctrine of God at either the undergraduate or the graduate level. The more I learned about this focus of the ancient church, the more I became convinced that the Trinity had to be our starting point in talking about God. And when we talk about the Trinity we are in the realm of the personal and relational.

My college and seminary classes had taught me that the most basic attribute of God was holiness, by which was meant absolute moral purity. That was the essence of God. However, I discovered as I learned Hebrew exegesis that while God is in fact described as holy in Scripture, the biblical concept of holiness was related to "set-apartness"—to God's transcendence, his "otherness," rather than his moral purity. In the Old Testament we have such diverse things as pans, chamber pots, and prostitutes described as holy—so whatever "holy" is, it is something other than moral rectitude. Over the years I have revisited the concept of holiness and become convinced that the term is related to the concept of wholeness.[6]

How has the church gone so wrong on this point? In the late second and early third centuries Tertullian left indelible fingerprints on all of Western theological understanding. He is remembered as the "Father of Latin Theology." It was Tertullian who first contributed to the development of the doctrine of the Trinity the insistence that God was "three persons, one substance" (*tres Personae, una Substantia*). However, Tertullian was a lawyer; he thought and taught in legal categories and terms, and in so doing laid down the tracks on which Western theology has run for the past 1,700+ years; in fact, New Testament scholar Gordon Fee has called Tertullian the "ultimate legalist."[7] In his wake the biblically revealed concept of covenant relationship was replaced by conceptions arising out of Roman jurisprudence. To use the phraseology of James B. Torrance, the West exchanged the biblical *covenant God* for a *contract God*.[8] The account of the incarnation was accordingly reframed

---

6. For a treatment of holiness as relational and Trinitarian, see John Webster, *Holiness* (Grand Rapids: Eerdmans, 2003). For a fine treatment of the concepts of legal and moral "holiness" versus wholeness as related to the believer's spiritual experience, see Donald Sloat, *Growing up Holy and Wholly* (Brentwood, TN: Wolgemuth & Hyatt, 1990). For our purposes, Sloat's study graphically demonstrates the failure of the "holiness teaching" that insists on holiness as moral perfection because God is holy. This doctrine as taught within Christianity has produced just the opposite of what is promised. Rather than freedom, joy, and peace, it produces guilt, defeat, and more sinful acts. One of the classic tests of truth is existential viability: does the "truth" work when put into practice in the concrete realities of life? If it does not, it must be rejected, no matter how good, honorable, noble, and even "holy" it sounds.

7. Gordon Fee, "Galatians in a Week," audio recording (http://www.gordonfeeonline.com/).

8. See James B. Torrance, *Worship Community and the Triune God of Grace* (Downers Grove, IL: InterVarsity Press, 1996), 95. Torrance also delves further into this idea in two articles he has published: "Covenant or Contract: A Study of the Theological Background of Worship in Seventeenth Century Scotland," *Scottish Journal of Theology* 23 (1970): 52–76, and "The Covenant Concept in Scottish Theology and Politics and Its Legacy," *Scottish Journal of Theology* 34 (1981): 225–43. See also his audio lectures available through Perichoresis.org: "Prayer and the Triune God of Grace" (http://www.perichoresis.org/store.html#!/~/product/category=1969362&id=8460487).

against the background of law, guilt, punishment, and restitution. The issue became *sins* as opposed to *sin*, deeds as opposed to heart condition, and the work of atonement was reframed as payment for our rebellion and failings, to the exclusion of healing and the re-creation of humanity in the image of the last Adam (Christ)—a theme that, by contrast, has remained at the center of Eastern Orthodox understanding.

To look at this issue from a different perspective, a couple of illustrations may prove helpful. Novelist John Steinbeck provides us with a vivid picture from a fishing expedition he took in the late 1940s that has immediate application to the present discussion:

> The Mexican sierra has "X-VII-15-IX" spines in the dorsal fin. These can be easily counted. But if the sierra strikes hard on the line so that our hands are burned, if the fish sounds and nearly escapes and finally comes in over the rail, his colors pulsing and his tail beating the air, *a whole new relation of externality has come into being—an entity which is more than the sum of the fish plus the fisherman.*
>
> The only way to count the spines of the sierra unaffected by this second relational reality is to sit in a laboratory, open an evil-smelling jar, remove a stiff colorless fish from formalin solution, count the spines and write the truth "D. XVII-15-IX." *There you have recorded a reality which cannot be assailed—probably the least important reality concerning either the fish or yourself.*[9]

In a similar vein, I am a great fan of both *CSI* and *NCIS*. Both television shows deal in criminal forensics, and in nearly every episode we find a murder. If there is a murder, there is an autopsy. We are brought into the autopsy room as the pathologist examines the body of the deceased to find the cause of death.

What do these illustrations have to do with our understanding of God? Actually, quite a lot. In an autopsy or by studying a book on anatomy we encounter the structure of the human body (or the fish). We see its various parts. We examine them individually, and we learn quite a

---

9. John Steinbeck and Edward F. Ricketts, *The Sea of Cortez* (New York: Penguin, 2009), 2. Italics added.

bit about how we as human beings are put together (or how the fish is). But if in our study of God we dissect him and split him up into various parts, do we really get to know him? No! God is personal and relational! We no more learn about the personal nature of God by examining his attributes than we learn about the person and life of the murder victim on the autopsy table by his or her dissection. I am not saying that looking at the attributes of God is unimportant, but I contend that this is at best a distant second when trying to apprehend, let alone comprehend, however imperfectly, who God is.

In our tradition, we Western Christians have focused our attention on the existence and attributes of God, especially his "holiness" (read moral or legal purity) and transcendence, and in practice downplayed if not downright ignored the importance of God as Trinity. A look at any standard systematic theology reveals a startling reality: roughly three times as much space is devoted to the existence and attributes of God as is spent in discussion of the Trinity. The seventeenth-century Puritan theologian Stephen Charnock wrote more than eight hundred pages on *The Existence and Attributes of God* without devoting even a single chapter to the Trinity! Surely the Trinity has something to do with the existence of God!

The net effect of this mentality is subtly and, I believe, unintentionally, to lead us to look for the "deeper reality" of God *behind* his self-revelation as Trinity.[10] The message, by means of treatment and arrangement, is that if we are to know God we need to probe into his essence, as though, since we cannot *really* know him personally, the best we can do is to examine each of his qualities in turn. The resulting picture of God is more closely related to the transcendent untouchable god of Plato, or to Aristotle's "unmoved mover," than to the dynamically relational Trinitarian persons revealed in Scripture by word and action. As the Puritan preacher and theologian Jonathan Edwards stated:

> The apostle tells us that "God is love"; and therefore, seeing he is an infinite being, it follows that he is an infinite fountain of

---

10. See Colin Gunton, *The Promise of Trinitarian Theology* (New York: T & T Clark, 1997), 30–55, for a discussion of Augustine's approach to the Trinity and his attempt to find the deeper truth about God behind the Trinity.

love. Seeing he is an all-sufficient being, it follows that he is a full and overflowing, and inexhaustible fountain of love. And in that he is an unchangeable and eternal being, he is an unchangeable and eternal fountain of love.[11]

Love is by definition other-centered. In the case of God, the incarnation is proof that God's love pours out of the Trinitarian persons' love for one another into other-centered, altruistic, and unconditional love for humanity. *The deepest truth of the divine being is the dynamic relationship of the love of the Father, Son, and Spirit.*

Karl Rahner describes the relationship between studying God's attributes and centering on the Trinity by using the example of the relationship between Aquinas's treatises *On the One God* and *On the Triune God*. He notes that the origins of this division entered in the wake of the work of Augustine, who began his examination of the person of God by looking at the concept of God's unity or oneness and only then moved to the individual persons. However, even as late as the work of Peter Lombard (d. 1160), who wrote *The Sentences*, the general doctrine of God was still subsumed under the heading of the Trinity. Beginning with Thomas Aquinas (d. 1274) we see a full-blown conceptual divide that seeks the essence of God *behind* the Trinitarian persons. The temptation then became to set up this essence as a fourth reality pre-existing the Trinitarian persons, to which the Trinity is only penultimate. Rahner notes that this theological method results in abstract and philosophical discussions about God that have virtually nothing to do with salvation history. "It speaks of the necessary metaphysical properties of God, and not very explicitly of God as experienced in salvation history in his free relations to his creatures."[12] He continues by noting that if the study of God begins with a non-Trinitarian treatise on the one God, it produces mere formal statements about the nature of the Trinity when it eventually turns its attention to that subtopic.[13] This is the very criticism made by Colin Gunton: any discussion of the

---

11. Jonathan Edwards, *Charity and Its Fruits* (reprint; Edinburgh: The Banner of Truth Trust, 1982), 327.
12. Rahner, *The Trinity*, 18.
13. Ibid.

Trinity that is not grounded in the incarnation floats off into abstract speculation.[14]

Those of us who have grown up in Western culture find the concrete personhood of the individual so central to our understanding that we cannot imagine how unknown it was to the ancients. In the cultural and philosophical substructure of the Greco-Roman world there was a presupposition that God and the world were an unbreakable unity in which there was no true freedom. It was in the Trinitarian debates, culminating in the Nicene pronouncements on the Trinity, that the modern understanding of personhood and personal freedom was born![15]

Reflecting on the Nicene discussions, John Zizioulas insists that "love as God's mode of existence 'hypostasizes' God, constitutes His being."

> The expression "God is love" (1 John 4:16) signifies that God "subsists" as Trinity, that is, as person not as substance. Love is not an emanation or "property" of the substance of God . . . but is *constitutive* of His substance, i.e., it is that which makes God what He is, the one God. Thus love ceases to be a qualifying—i.e., secondary—property of being and becomes the supreme ontological predicate. Love as God's mode of existence "hypostatizes" God, *constitutes* His being.[16]

To state this more simply: it is the interrelation of the divine persons of the Trinity that makes God the being that God is.

Coming back to what I was taught: if we imagine that holiness (particularly as commonly understood) or any other attribute is more fundamental to God's being than the relationality of the Trinitarian persons in love, it profoundly affects the way we relate to God. Everything

---

14. "In considering the relation of Christology to Trinitarian theology, two distinct considerations must be held in mind. The first is that some account of the divinity of the historical Christ is a necessary condition of the Christian Trinity, as distinct from some merely rational triad. The second is that a firm hold on the material humanity of the incarnate son is a prerequisite for a doctrine of the Trinity that does not float off into abstraction from the concrete history of salvation" (Gunton, *The Promise of Trinitarian Theology*, 34).

15. See John D. Zizioulas, *Being as Communion* (New York: St. Vladimir's Seminary Press, 1985), 27–65.

16. Ibid., 46.

changes if we think of the relationship of the Father, Son, and Spirit as simply a characteristic, or one among many characteristics of God, and not the fundamental reality of divine being. Take holiness again: *if relationship is not the deepest truth of God's being, then the holiness of God is not a relational concept at all.*[17]

The path to knowing God is through Jesus. If we place any kind of wedge between Jesus and the Father we commit a serious error. (Is "heresy" too strong a word here?) Philip asked Jesus to "show us the Father." Jesus' reply was, "Whoever has seen me has seen the Father" (John 14:8–9). In the opening chapter of his Gospel, John says that no one has seen God (the Father) at any time. The only-begotten Son/God[18] who is in the bosom of the Father, he has explained (literally, "exegeted") him, has shown who he is (1:18).

God as Trinity exists in an eternal dynamic relationship of self-giving love. Daniel Migliore has noted:

> When we speak of God as three persons, we are not to understand three individual selves isolated and independent, but three subsistences who derive their personal identity from the dynamic interpersonal relationship in which they exist. Their "realities are defined by intersubjectivity, shared consciousness, faithful relationships, and the mutual giving and receiving of love."[19]

Unpacking the Nicene-Constantinopolitan Creed (381)

We believe in one God, the Father Almighty,
Maker of heaven and earth, and of all things visible and invisible;
And in one Lord Jesus Christ, the Son of God, the Only-begotten,
Begotten of the Father before all ages, Light of Light,
Very God of Very God,

---

17. For a treatment of holiness as relational and Trinitarian, see Webster, *Holiness.*

18. There is a textual problem here: some important manuscripts read "only-begotten Son," while other important manuscripts read "only-begotten God."

19. Daniel L. Migliore, *Faith Seeking Understanding* (Grand Rapids: Eerdmans, 1991), 68.

Begotten, not made; of one essence with the Father,
by whom all things were made:
Who for us men and for our salvation came down from heaven,
and was incarnate of the Holy Spirit and the Virgin Mary,
and was made man;
And was crucified also for us under Pontius Pilate,
and suffered and was buried;
And the third day He rose again,
according to the Scriptures;
And ascended into heaven,
and sits at the right hand of the Father;
And He shall come again with glory
to judge the living and the dead,
Whose kingdom shall have no end.
And we believe in the Holy Spirit, the Lord, and Giver of Life,
Who proceeds from the Father,
Who with the Father and the Son together is worshiped and glorified,
Who spoke by the Prophets;
And we believe in one, holy, catholic, and apostolic church.
We acknowledge one Baptism for the remission of sins.
We look for the Resurrection of the dead,
And the Life of the age to come. Amen.

"We Believe in One God the Father"

When we read the first line of the creed, the assertion is so generally accepted that we may wonder why the council even penned this line. It seems self-evident. In reality, while this statement is utterly non-controversial to us, the Arian heresy against which the creed was written denied this fundamental Christian understanding. As noted in the previous chapter, Arius held to a Neoplatonic cosmology or worldview. This worldview was fundamentally dualistic and drew a sharp distinction between the created material universe, subject to constant change, decay, and death, and the uncreated changeless spiritual realm. The depraved material universe was placed in opposition to the eternal spiritual reality, which was permanent, calm, and unchanging. This was the realm of the intelligible, of the eternal ideas, untouched by the ebb and flow of material existence. It was the realm in which God dwelt. The finite realm of the material, with its welter of fleeting sense impressions, could not be as valuable or as valid as the realm of the ideas, the spiritual, the perfect; hence the goal was to escape from the former into the latter.

God was eternal, spirit and alone, an undivided monad, absolute and non-relational and ultimately unknowable. He was so transcendent he was sometimes described as "beyond being" itself. He could not directly touch the material world, and could not have created the material order. Instead, he created the Word/*Logos*, a created spiritual being who in turn created the material world and all that it contained. Arius therefore asserted that God the "unoriginate" had not always been Father; only when he created the Word/*Logos* by an act of his will did he become Father, and even then he was Father by adoption only because the Son was not innately related to him and did not share his being—was not, as it were, of God's own DNA, but only a powerful and beautiful creature.

As Athanasius, the fourth-century bishop of Alexandria, said in refutation of Arius's heresy: "[It] will be much more accurate to denote God from the Son and to call Him Father, than to name Him and call Him unoriginate from His works only; for the latter term refers to the works that have come to be at the will of God through the Word, but the name of Father points out the proper offspring from His essence."[20] In other words, by identifying God primarily as "unoriginate," Arius was defining him by reference to those things that *are* "originate," the things God has made, rather than by reference to God's own being, namely, his relation to the Son.

Read in its original context, then, the opening statement of the creed is astonishing in its own right. It asserts that God is first Father, then creator. He did not become Father; his eternal identity is found in his fatherhood. Moreover, since "Father" is a term of personhood as well as relationality, the early church fathers recognized that God was first and foremost personal, and a divine person in relationship. He is Father—and by implication Son—even before creation, and that relationship between the Father and the Son is the relationship under discussion in the creed. It is a relationship of *homoousia*: sameness of essence or being. In the decades after Nicaea the implications of this reality were developed.

---

20. Athanasius, *Select Works and Letters* 7:39, in *Nicene and Post-Nicene Fathers, Second Series*, vol. 4, ed. Philip Schaff (Grand Rapids: Eerdmans, 1975), 325.

In the debates with the Arians following the Council of Nicaea, Athanasius, reflecting more deeply on the being of God, states explicitly that the term "Father," like the term "God," signifies the "essence" of God. (In another place he says the same thing about "Son.") In other words, the term "Father" (like the term "Son") reflects "nothing other than a genuine intimation of the nature of God's being."[21] As Athanasius himself states, "If God be simple, as he is, it follows that in naming Him Father we are not saying something about God, but signifying his essence itself."[22] Fatherhood (as well as sonship) is, according to Athanasius, part of what makes God who he is.[23]

To lift this concept out of its original context of debate with Arianism and state it positively, and to extend this further: he is a dynamic tri-personal relationship of love.

"Almighty" (Pantocrator)

I must say a few words about the concept behind the word "Almighty." As children, many of us were taught the song that begins, "God can do anything, anything, anything; God can do anything but fail."

When I was in high school, I learned the trio of attributes—omniscient, omnipotent, and omnipresent. I was challenged by a classmate, "If God can do anything, can he make a square circle?" When I have asked my students this question, I have often received the answer, "Of course! God can do anything." It is not hard to recognize that this is a trick question involving a logical category error. It does bring us up short, however, forcing us to ask what is meant when we say that God can do anything because God is omnipotent, or what it means that he is in control of all. Again, when pressed, many have taken this to deny that there is any contingency in creation: that God *causes* all things directly or indirectly.

The problem is that this kind of thinking is speculative and abstract, operating on the assumption that God's omnipotence is simply like our power raised to the nth degree. It conceives of divine power as arbitrary

---

21. Peter Widdicombe, *The Fatherhood of God from Origen to Athanasius* (Oxford: Clarendon, 1994), 172.

22. Ibid.

23. Ibid, citing Athanasius, Opitz. 18:21–31.

and loses touch with God's actual, concrete demonstration of his power in history.[24] Hilary of Poitiers (ca. 300–ca. 368) insists that God's omnipotence must not be conceived of as what we think he can do, but must be defined by what he has done and continues to do in Jesus Christ. In other words, his almightiness is demonstrated in humility and condescension, particularly in the incarnation. God's almighty power is not demonstrated by coercion, by untold legions of angels and mighty armies conquering. It is rather demonstrated in self-emptying, the "foolishness" of the incarnation and the cross: that is how he carried out his most momentous work of transformative reconciliation.[25]

"Creator of All Things Visible and Invisible"

The second phrase of the creed is also a direct attack on Arianism, declaring that it is the eternal Father himself who is in a real and vital sense directly involved in creation.

> God, who needs nothing, loves into existence wholly superfluous creatures in order that He may love and perfect them.[26]
> —C. S. LEWIS

Creation did not come out of boredom, loneliness, or necessity. The divine Trinity is complete and self-sufficient. The decision to create arose entirely out of divine freedom rather than any external or intrinsic necessity. Despite the rationale popular in some Christian quarters, I believe even the conclusion that God created "in order to show forth his glory" fails because ultimately that would reflect some need within the godhead. That there is any lack in God is unthinkable. Paul testifies to this in Acts 17:24–25:

---

24. Thomas F. Torrance, *The Trinitarian Faith*, 82.

25. Hilary of Poitiers, *On the Trinity*, book 1, 13–19, In *The Nicene and Post-Nicene Fathers*, vol. 9, ed. Philip Schaff (Grand Rapids: Eerdmans, 1975). See 1 Corinthians 1:25.

26. C.S. Lewis, *The Four Loves* (New York: Harcourt Brace & Co, 1960), 127.

The God who made the world and everything in it, who is Lord of heaven and earth, does not live in temples made by human hands, nor is he served by human hands, as if he needed anything, because he himself gives life and breath and everything to everyone.

Creation was not based on any lack within the godhead. He gains nothing from our existence; in fact, the decision to create was infinitely costly to God. The only explanation for there being anything at all outside God himself is that God is love. Love is creative and expansive. Love is generous. Creation must be grounded in the love of God that desires to share relationship beyond the perfection of triune love, just as redemption is grounded in the self-giving love of God. Or to put it in the words of Douglas Fairbairn, "The relationship between the persons of the Trinity was so valuable that God created people in his image to share in that relationship."[27] In a similar vein C. S. Lewis has observed:

In God there is no hunger that needs to be filled; only plenteousness that desires to give. The doctrine that God was under no necessity to create is not a piece of dry scholastic speculation. It is essential. Without it we can hardly avoid the conception of what I can only call a "managerial" God; a Being whose function or nature is to "run" the universe, who stands to it as a head-master to a school. . . . But to be sovereign of the universe is no great matter to God. In himself, at home in "the land of the Trinity," he is Sovereign of a far greater realm. We must keep always before our eyes that vision of Lady Julian's (Julian of Norwich) in which God carried in his hand a little object like a nut, and that nut was "all that is made." *God, who needs nothing, loves into existence wholly superfluous creatures in order that He may love and perfect them.*[28]

Likewise Thomas Torrance has observed, "[In] the unlimited freedom of his love, God created the world out of nothing, and did not grudge

---

27. Douglas Fairbairn, *Life in the Trinity: An Introduction to Theology with the Help of the Fathers* (Downers Grove, IL: InterVarsity Press, 2009), loc. 4756, Kindle ed.
28. C. S. Lewis, *The Four Loves* (New York: Harcourt Brace Jovanovich, 1960), 17.

bringing into being an altogether new reality utterly different from his own."[29] He continues:

> God is not limited by our feeble capacities or incapacities, but in his grace and outgoing love he graciously condescends to enter fellowship with us. . . . In his love of us and for us God freely wills not to be without us and wills to be with us as those whom he has eternally chosen to coexist with himself and share his eternal love. . . . He does not want to be alone without us or want us to be alone without him.[30]
>
> It is in the Cross of Christ that the utterly astonishing nature of the Love that God is has been fully disclosed, for in refusing to spare his own Son whom he delivered up for us all, God has revealed that *he loves us more than he loves himself.* And so it is in the Cross of Jesus Christ above all that God has exhibited the very Nature of his Being as Love and has irrevocably committed his Being to relationship with us in unconditional Love.[31]

To say that creation arose out of free divine decision, and not out of any necessity or obligation on God's part, is to say that creation is *contingent.* This in turn means that creation has a degree of freedom built into it. The creation is finite and dependent on God's free act, but it is not a part of him; he has given it genuine reality.

And he continues to do so. The created order has been created *ex nihilo*, "out of nothing"; this is hinted at in Genesis 1 and explicitly stated in Hebrews 11, but these passages do not address the fact that the created order does not continue to exist independently as a finished product apart from the creator's constant immanent care. Despite our experience of reality, it does not and cannot continue to exist on its own; it has no ongoing stability within itself. Its continued existence is by reason of the continuing sustaining activity of God, by the free

---

29. Thomas F. Torrance, *The Christian Doctrine of God: One Being, Three Persons* (Edinburgh: T & T Clark, 1996), 237. Though not for the faint-hearted, this work is utterly magnificent.

30. Ibid., 4.

31. Ibid., 5. Italics added.

act of the divine will. While for millennia humanity has held that the universe was eternal, the testimony of Scripture is that creation is finite and had an absolute beginning. Interestingly, the scientific community has been hauled to this conclusion more or less kicking and screaming against the evidence of the Big Bang, which points to an absolute finite beginning of the universe and hence the necessity of a creator of some sort.

God's relationship to the universe is neither necessary nor arbitrary. Existing as other than God, yet upheld by God, creation manifests a limited but real freedom.

Homoousios

The point of the Nicene Creed was to assert precisely and forcefully the eternal equality of the Father and the Son, and not leave any ground for Arianism. The term adopted in the creed was *homoousios*, meaning that the Father and the Son partake of the "same" (*homo* = "same, identical") "essence" (*ousia* = "being") and thus eliminating the possibility of asserting that God was ever singular and alone.

As noted earlier, Arianism arose out of an embedding of the revelation of the person and work of Christ within a Greco-Roman worldview rooted in cosmological philosophical concepts that were not just incompatible with the persons of the Father and the Son as revealed in their interactions with the world recorded in Scripture, but fundamentally opposed to that revelation. Athanasius in particular understood that should Arianism win, the gospel would be lost and Christianity would be reduced to morality. If Christianity were to survive, the understanding of an entire culture would have to be transformed.

The concept that the members of the Trinity are *homoousioi* with each other has several profound implications.

More than a century before the Council of Nicaea, Irenaeus (d. ca. 205) insisted that there had to be an eternal indivisible union between God the Father and the incarnate Son-mediator, Jesus Christ. The person and work of the Son give us a window of understanding into who God is inherently and eternally in himself. In other words, *if Jesus and the Father were not eternally united and he was somehow not totally one with the Father, we have no real assurance as to who God is in himself.* There might be a part of himself that he has withheld from the Son and therefore from us.[32] To put this another way, because the Father and the Son are eternally and inherently one, we can *know* God by looking at Jesus. In Jesus we see not just a part or aspect of God, but the totality of what it means to be God. As Thomas Torrance has said, "*There is no God behind the back of Jesus.*"[33] While it may be possible to know something *about* God by examining his creation, creation is not of the same essence or being as God; it is merely what he has made, as opposed to who he is.

The concept of *homoousia* also implies that the Son and the Father (and the Holy Spirit) are equal. During the early centuries before the Council of Nicaea there was a general recognition that Jesus was in some way God, but at the same time a regular assertion that the Son was somehow less God than the Father was. The technical term for this is "subordinationism." The difficulty here was that Scripture sometimes uses language that makes it clear that the Son is God, and yet at other times it appears that the Son is subordinate to the Father. This confusion was not sorted out until the early fathers came to recognize that statements about the Son's relation to the Father fell into two categories: on the one hand there were statements about Jesus' deity, which could not be denied, while on the other there were statements that spoke of the Son obeying the Father. The former were *ontological*—that is, statements of being—whereas the latter were *economic*—that is, statements relating to the "job description" of the incarnate Son (as God-man) in his work of redeemer. Once this distinction was understood, the full, equal, eternal, unsubordinated deity of the Son was recognized. Theologians have referred ever since to the *immanent* or *ontological Trinity* (the triune God as he is in himself) and the *economic Trinity* (the triune God as he relates to the world).

Theologically, the term *homoousios* rules out the idea of subordinationism. Ultimately the church came to understand the term as embodying the very essence of the gospel.[34]

---

32. See G. L. Prestige, *God in Patristic Thought* (London: Alec R. Allenson, 1952), 197–218.

33. Thomas F. Torrance, *The Doctrine of Jesus Christ* (Eugene OR: Wipf and Stock, 2002), 15.

34. Elmer M. Colyer, *How to Read T. F. Torrance* (Downers Grove, IL: InterVarsity Press, 2001), 72–73.

[The Nicene Creed] hinges upon the fact that he who became incarnate in Jesus Christ, he who mediates divine revelation and reconciliation to mankind in and through himself, is God of God, Light of Light, very God of very God—that is to say, Jesus Christ is to be acknowledged as God in the same sense as the Father is acknowledged as God, for it is in virtue of his Deity that his saving work as man has its validity.[35]

More will be said in subsequent chapters about exactly how the validity of Jesus' saving work depends on his deity.

Perichoresis

The life of God is a social life that becomes the source and example for community among God's creatures. The Trinitarian persons "indwell" each other (*perichoresis*), make room for each other, and are "hospitable" to each other, or, to use another metaphor, "they are united in an exquisite divine dance."[36] The term *perichoresis*, although not found in the Nicene Creed itself, became the technical term to describe the way the persons of the godhead relate to one another. The term comes from a combination of two Greek words: *peri* ("around") and *chorein* ("contain").

Love is something that one person has for another person. If God was a single person, then before the world was made, He was not love.
—C. S. LEWIS[37]

While the persons of the godhead are three, they are not individual persons in the same sense that we humans are isolated individuals. The three are one in essence or being, and in their respective personhoods indwell each other. "They fully contain each other as whole persons

---

35. Thomas F. Torrance, *The Mediation of Christ* (Colorado Springs, CO: Helmers and Howard, 1992), 54–55.

36. Migliore, *Faith Seeking Understanding,* 70.

37. C. S. Lewis, *Mere Christianity* (New York: Touchstone, 1996), 151.

without any diminishment to the honour and glory of one another."[38] There is not nor was there ever, nor could there ever be, any separation between them. While we human beings do not and cannot exist within each other, this is precisely the mode of the eternal existence of the tri-une God. According to John of Damascus (d. 749), they are like "three suns cleaving to one another without any separation and giving out their light combined and conjoined into one."[39]

While our conception of God is often that he is static, quietly sitting on his throne and receiving worship from creation, the concept of *perichoresis* tells us something very different. The divine reality is dynamic, not static; it is an interpenetrating of one another in a relational, spiritual, and intensely personal way. Theirs is a permanently shared consciousness. There is no secret part of any one member that is withheld from the others. As a lifelong *Star Trek* fan, I would liken (however imperfectly) the interpersonal relationships of the members of the Trinity to a permanent Vulcan mind-meld, where all the deepest thoughts and feelings are always open and on display to the parties of the joined consciousness.

To flesh this out a bit more, the relationship between the Father and the Son (and the Spirit) is one of rich and deep communion. The Father reveals himself fully to the Son. When we hear the term "revelation," we think of information, of propositions; but the Greek term translated "revelation" actually means "unveiling." This is not primarily information, but personal self-disclosure—the Father unveils himself to the Son. He gives himself, not information about himself, to the Son. Jesus is the only one to whom the Father has unveiled himself completely. He has told Moses and the other prophets about himself, and they have seen his action and written down his commandments and oracles, but these occasions do not involve a personal unveiling of his complete and innermost being. The prophets have had a genuine, but only limited, encounter with him.

---

38. Thomas F. Torrance, *The Christian Doctrine of God*, 169.

39. John of Damascus, *Exposition of the Orthodox Faith* I.VIII, in *Nicene and Post-Nicene Fathers, Second Series*, vol. 9, ed. Philip Schaff (Grand Rapids: Eerdmans, 1976), 11.

There is a face-to-face communion between the Father and the Son that is utterly unique. *No one* knows the Father but the Son. This knowledge is profound and personal. The Father discloses all he is to the Son, and vice versa. This is direct, complete personal knowledge of the Father by the Son and of the Son by the Father. Others have known about God, they have even known him to an extent, but they have not known him fully and completely. Jesus has a *complete, thorough,* and *unfiltered* knowledge of the Father as he is in himself, in his innermost being. While the prophet Isaiah can proclaim, "Truly, you are a God who hides himself, O God of Israel, Savior!" (Isa. 45:15), between Jesus and the Father *nothing* is hidden.

As I said earlier, this is a closed circle of knowing—one that is so close, so intimate, so personal, so complete, as to an exchange of souls, an unbounded *koinonia* (communion). This knowledge is so complete and so intimate that any other level of knowledge does not even qualify as knowledge by comparison. This is a dynamic relationship of self-disclosure and encounter in love. John reflects this in the opening verse of his Gospel: "In the beginning was the Word, and the Word was with [*pros*, "face to face with"] God and the Word was God" (1:1). John repeats the idea even more forcefully in 1:18: "The only-begotten God who is in the bosom of the Father, he has made him known."

The Gospels testify to the Father's delight in the Son: "You are my beloved Son in whom my soul delights."[40] This is a relationship not only of knowledge and self-revelation, but also of mutual love and delight. Jesus, too, loves the Father with all his heart, soul, mind, and strength. This love relationship is personal encounter and communion of the most intimate and profound kind. It is a self-giving love.

The relationship between Father and Son is so intense and personal and complete that Jesus says he is *in* the Father and the Father is *in* him. We can wish for such profound intimacy, but it is so far beyond our experience that we cannot begin to truly imagine its overwhelming, mind-boggling beauty. It is *perichoresis*: mutual interpenetration, indwelling, union. The persons of the Trinity pass into one another and contain one another in a relationship so close and intertwined that to

---

40. Conflation of Matthew 3:17, 12:18, and 17:5.

behold Jesus is to behold the Father (John 12:44). Yet there is still distinction: Jesus says "I and the Father are one," not "I am the Father."

As profound and indescribable as this self-giving love relationship is, it is not narcissistic, nor is it hoarding. Rather, it is focused outwardly, toward *us*.

> The Father, Son and Spirit love us *for our benefit*, not for increasing their membership rolls, or for making themselves look good, or for anything they can get from us. There is no need in the blessed Trinity. It is an overflowing fountain of other-centered love. The shared life of the Father, Son and Spirit is about giving, not taking; sharing, not hoarding; blessing others with life for their sakes, not manipulating for divine control. The Father, Son, and Spirit are focused upon giving themselves for our benefit, so that we too can experience real life. They need nothing in return.[41]

The twelfth-century mystical theologian Richard of St. Victor (d. 1165) wrote a profound work titled *On the Trinity*, in which he seeks to prove the necessity of the Trinity rather than just accepting it on the authority of the church. Starting with the unequivocal statement that "God is love," he argues that this in itself proves that God in his personhood cannot be an eternal monad because love in its highest expression cannot be alone. He says, "No one is properly said to have charity [Christian love, i.e., *agape*] on the basis of his own private love of himself. And so it is necessary for love to be directed toward another person for it to be charity. Therefore, where a plurality of persons is lacking, charity cannot exist."[42] Without an object outside the self, love becomes narcissism. God must be at least two persons, each of whom loves another person as the object of that love.

But Richard does not stop there. He goes on to insist that love in its highest form requires the two who love one another to be united in the

---

41. C. Baxter Kruger, *The Shack Revisited: There Is More Going On Here Than You Ever Dared to Dream* (New York: Faith Works, 2012), 120.

42. Richard of St. Victor, *Richard of St Victor*, trans. Grover Zinn (New York: Paulist 1979), 374–75.

common love of a third. For example, two parents are united in love for their child, who is the object of their combined love. It is only in this way that love is perfect.

In the early sixth century Boethius (d. 525)[43] defined a person as "an individual substance of a nature endowed with reason."[44] This concept of personhood reflects a radical individuality and separateness for each person. What is fascinating is that while Boethius's definition still holds sway in popular culture, psychologists and therapists beginning with William James in the late nineteenth century have come to recognize that one's identity as a person is defined and constituted by one's relationships. This makes perfect sense if humanity, as the apex of creation (even in its radically fallen condition), profoundly reflects who God is. What I am suggesting is in line with the thought of Richard of St. Victor: that the persons of the godhead are defined by their perfect and interpersonal dynamic relationships. This concept is itself a further development of both Athanasius and the Cappadocians.

Thomas Torrance insists that we be "scientific" rather than speculative in our theological methodology. By this he means that we must examine things in their intrinsic relationships, and then from that study draw our conclusions. With reference to the relationship of the persons of the Trinity, he concludes:

> The relations which persons have with one another as persons are onto-relations, for they are person-constituting relations. That was a concept and a way of thinking developed through the understanding of the Holy Trinity as a Communion of Love in whom Father, Son and Holy Spirit mutually involve and co-inhere[45] in one another in the profound onto-relations of that Communion, without any blurring of their hypostatic distinctions or properties as Father, Son and Holy Spirit which

---

43. Boethius, sometimes regarded as the last Roman as well as a significant philosopher, wrote *De Consolatione Philosophiae*. Throughout the Middle Ages he was regarded as a martyr for the Christian faith, but contemporary scholars see his death as politically motivated by his king, who suspected him of treason. He did remain devoted to his faith to the end, even if his death was not due to his Christian faith.

44. John Marenbon, *Boethius* (New York: Oxford University Press, 2003), 72.

45. That is, inhere or exist together, as in one substance.

would make them no more than modal aspects in an undifferentiated oneness of divine Being.[46]

Hierarchy or Equality?

One more vital issue needs to be addressed by way of implications of the
homoousion, as the concept of sameness of being has come to be called
(using the form of the word that appears in the creed). As pointed out
above, when the Nicene Creed is unpacked, it unequivocally rules out
the concept of an eternal hierarchy within the Trinity. To even suggest
this violates the concepts of *homoousia* and *perichoresis*. The idea of a
hierarchy, where one of the divine persons is "in charge," introduces the
ancient error of subordinationism into our concept of God.

Let us comfort ourselves in the thought
of the Father and Son. So long as there dwells
harmony, so long as the Son loves the Father
with all the love the Father can welcome,
all is well with the little ones.
—GEORGE MACDONALD[47]

Yet we are seeing just such a move within evangelicalism today, arising out of conflicts over gender relations. Several high-profile evangelical theologians, including some who are leaders in the Evangelical
Theological Society, have attempted to link the issue of hierarchical
ordered gender roles to an eternal hierarchy in the Trinity. If there is
hierarchy in the Trinity, then hierarchy is at the foundation and ground
of personal existence—inherent in the godhead and therefore inherent
in humanity as bearing God's image.

This, I am convinced, is a grave error, and I am not alone in thinking
so. What is most disturbing is that the arguments used to defend this
view are the same as those used by the Arians in the fourth century to

---

46. Thomas F. Torrance, *The Mediation of Christ*, 49.

47 George MacDonald, *Creation in Christ: Unspoken Sermons*, ed. Roland Hein
(Vancouver: Regent College, 1976), 22.

argue that Christ was not in fact God. In his book *Who's Tampering with the Trinity?*[48] Millard Erickson concludes that while both sides of the argument—the egalitarians and the hierarchicalists—commit several logical fallacies in their argumentation, the hierarchicalists are drawing conclusions that cut at the very heart of the nature of God and hence the heart of Christianity itself. While denying that the hierarchicalists have crossed the line into Arianism, he nevertheless sternly warns that their students may well cross that line. In my opinion, Erickson is not overreacting. In the history of theology we can see over and over again that students work out the implicit propositions of their mentors, and go where their mentors would not go. We pay a price for our ignorance of the most foundational doctrines and realities of the faith.

> In God there is no hunger that needs to be filled,
> only plenteousness that desires to give.
> —C. S. Lewis[49]

---

48. Millard J. Erickson, *Who's Tampering with the Trinity?* (Grand Rapids: Kregel, 2009).

49. Lewis, *The Four Loves*, 126.

Chapter 5

The Son of the Father

Introduction: Who Is Jesus?

There is an old story about a man who went to a building site. Coming upon a worker, he asked him what he was doing, and the worker replied, "I'm laying bricks."

The man moved a few steps farther and found another worker to whom he posed the same question: "What are you doing?" This time the reply was: "I'm building a wall."

A little farther on in the construction site he found yet a third worker and asked him the same question. The worker answered, "I'm helping Sir Christopher Wren build St. Paul's Cathedral."

All three men gave true answers, and yet each answer was considerably different. The difference in the answers is perspective. And perspective makes all the difference in the world as to how we see things.

Over the past roughly four hundred years we have seen an incredible shift in perspective with reference to the identity of Jesus Christ. Alisdar Heron has observed, "At the peak of the Middle Ages around the year 1200, Christianity was more or less solidly established as the religion of Europe . . . and theology was regarded—and not only by theologians—as the 'queen of the sciences,' the supreme intellectual discipline."[1] Throughout Europe before the Enlightenment, the

---

1. Alisdair Heron, *A Century of Protestant Theology* (Philadelphia: Westminster, 1980), 1.

position of Jesus Christ was understood to be one of cosmic lordship over both the spiritual and political realms; ultimately even the kings of the earth were subject to him. But for a host of reasons we do not have time to get into, the next several centuries witnessed what I would call *the incredible shrinking of Jesus.* European civilization under the influence of the Enlightenment cast off the shackles of authority on which society had been established: the authority of kings, of the church, of the Scriptures, and of Jesus Christ and God. The ultimate appeal for truth became human reason. The position of Jesus shrank from that of cosmic lordship to that of simply another questionable authority among many. But the shrinking did not end there. Ultimately, the vision of Jesus we have inherited today is one that is strictly "spiritual," that belongs to the realm of "faith" and is unrelated to the larger created order: science, politics, economics, the arts, or any kind of public discourse. Jesus has been relegated to our private internal spiritual experience. His name is not mentioned in polite society. Interestingly, it was this very attitude of cultured society in Berlin that compelled Friedrich Schleiermacher to pen *On Religion: Speeches to its Cultured Despisers* in 1799.

At this point I ask a question that has been asked before. "Can we overestimate Jesus Christ? Can we make too much of his identity, his personhood, and his cosmic claims?" In the words of C. Baxter Kruger: "Is it possible to give Jesus a place in our theological vision that is over the top, so to speak, too significant, too critical, too central? Can we make too much of Christ? Can we give him a role in the creation and in the purpose of the cosmos that is far more than he is actually worthy of? Are we in error if we make Jesus Christ our fundamental hermeneutic (interpretive principle)? Are we in error if we make our hermeneutical glasses Christological glasses?"[2]

These are not mere rhetorical questions. Theological traditions over the centuries have taken many twists and turns. As noted in chapter 1, many divergent issues—often becoming theological hobbyhorses—have been placed at the center of the various traditions. Catholicism puts the church and sacraments at the center; Lutheranism, justification

---

2. C. Baxter Kruger, "Is Jesus a Footnote to Adam? http://baxterkruger.blogspot.com/2008/01/is-jesus-footnote-to-adam.html

by faith; Reformed theology, the sovereignty of God; Arminianism, human freedom; Wesleyanism, holiness; Dispensationalism, eschatology; Pentecostalism, the gifts of the Spirit.

I could go on, but I think the point has been made. Each of these traditions takes a piece of the truth and makes that piece the lens through which all theological understanding is focused. Whatever doesn't fit is marginalized—left on the "cutting-room floor," as it were. In the process, God himself in his Trinitarian personhood fades into the background. In particular, the astonishing reality of the incarnation, motivated by God's incomprehensible gracious love for humanity and revealing the humility and other-centeredness of the Father, Son, and Spirit, disappears from view. Yet it is the reality of this self-giving love of God that sets Christianity apart from every other religion in the history of the world.

God himself, out of infinite love and compassion, has humbled himself to become one of us in order to draw us to himself. We only have to open the Gospel of John to come face to face with this astonishing reality. John recounts several incredible statements that Jesus made about himself: "I am the way, the truth, and the life" (14:6), "I am the light of the world" (8:12), and others. The apostle records seven of these "I am" statements (6:35; 8:12; 10:9; 10:11; 11:25; 14:6; 15:1).

For that was the very purpose and end of our
Lord's Incarnation, that He should join what is man
by nature to Him who is by nature God.[3]
—ATHANASIUS

In the following pages, we look at who Jesus is as revealed in Scripture. By its very nature this will be a limited survey: the apostle John said that if everything Jesus did and taught were to be written down, the world itself could not contain the volumes that would be written (21:25). Our task here is to look intently at Jesus' core identity.

---

3. Athanasius *The Orations of St. Athanasius against the Arians*, in *The Nicene and Post-Nicene Fathers*, vol. 2, 70, edited by Philip Schaff (Grand Rapids: Eerdmans, 1975).

For most of us, when we think of Jesus, our thoughts are drawn to Christmas, with images of shepherds, wise men, a stable with a manger and the baby, and angels singing "Peace on Earth." In short, we focus mainly on Jesus' birth and his subsequent life on earth, ending in his crucifixion and resurrection. We affirm that he is God, but don't stop to unpack the specific biblical affirmations about him and their implications. In truth, Jesus is more central to reality than we can ever imagine. As Papa says in *The Shack*, "Creation and history are all about Jesus. He is the very center of our purpose."[4]

In this chapter we begin to unpack the significance of Jesus as he is presented in several key scriptural images and identifications that speak of who he is in his person as opposed to what he did. In particular we focus on three overriding relationships:

- The eternal Son of the Father and second person of the Trinity
- Lord of creation: the creator and sustainer of everything that exists
- The Anointed One

The Father's Son

Who is Jesus? We can read the Gospels and make a list of all the names and titles of Jesus and all the things that Jesus did, all the miracles he performed. We can expand this list of names and titles in the Gospels to include those in the prophets as well. Such a list would give a biblical picture of Jesus insofar as all of these names and titles are explicitly stated in Scripture, but even if we were so meticulous as to find every name and title, we would still be in danger of missing the point. We are so familiar with the text, and have read it so many times through the grid we have absorbed, that we miss one of the most obvious titles and the underlying identity from which virtually all the other names and titles are derived: *Son*. This title and the relationship it denotes make Jesus absolutely and utterly unique, qualitatively different from any other person in human history. In Jesus, the Father's eternal Son has come to us. This

---

4. William P. Young, *The Shack* (Newbury Park, CA: Windblown Media, 2008), loc. 209, Kindle ed.

is where the apostle John starts his Gospel: the only-begotten Son who is in the bosom of the Father has explained the Father (1:18).[5]

We miss the point because we are so accustomed to calling God "Father" that we do not recognize how blasphemous this sounded to first-century Jews. There is no evidence anywhere in Scripture or in rabbinic literature of any Jew ever personally addressing God as Father. In John 8, the Jews try to stone Jesus for calling God his Father. The Jews recognized that this was a claim to deity! While we do find God referred to as "Father" fifteen times in the Old Testament, these references refer to God as the Father of Israel (or to Israel as God's son) or of the Davidic king (who was seen to be God's adopted son). These references are never personal (with respect to whoever is thought of as the son) or ontological.

In other words, the concept of the fatherhood of God, while not completely absent from the Old Testament, was at best in the background of Israel's understanding. The New Testament presents a sharp, and from the Jewish perspective blasphemous, contrast to the Old Testament. When we open the pages of the New Testament we find that the landscape has been transformed. While God is referred to as "Father" 15 times in the entire Old Testament, we find this name for God used more than 100 times in the Gospel of John alone, mostly by Jesus himself. In all four Gospels together, God is referred to as "Father" 179 times.

While no first-century Jew would dare address God as "Father," this was exactly what Jesus did regularly, incurring the wrath of the establishment.[6] He even taught his disciples to do the same! When the disciples entreated the Savior to teach them to pray, he responded, "Pray this way: 'Our Father who is in heaven'" (Matt. 6:9; Luke 11:1–2). The

---

5. There is a textual problem in this verse. Should the reading be "the only-begotten God" or "the only-begotten Son"? This is a difficult decision. For a technical discussion of the textual evidence, see https://net.bible.org/#!bible/John+1:16.

6. Jeremias has stated, ". . . I have examined the prayer literature of ancient Judaism—a large, rich literature, all too little explored. The result of the examination was that in no place in this immense literature is this invitation of God as Father to be found. . . . No Jew would have dared to address God in this manner. Jesus did always, in all his prayers which are handed down to us, with one single exception, the cry from the cross: "My God, my God, why hast thou forsaken me?" (Joachim Jeremias, *The Prayers of Jesus* [Minneapolis: Fortress, 1978], 97).

apostle Paul goes more than a step further. He says that God is our *Abba*, an Aramaic term that has the depth of emotional intimacy of "Dad" or "Daddy": hardly the solemn and formal reverence that most of us have been taught. This is an intimate family relationship, a term that presupposes the closest of loving and caring familial bonds between us individually and our heavenly Father.

While we regularly hear from those of a more liberal theological persuasion that we are all sons and daughters of God and that Jesus was just an especially pious man who maintained a particularly close relationship with God, the testimony of the New Testament and the early church is radically different. Jesus was not just a man who was arbitrarily picked by YHWH out of many potential candidates. He alone possessed a unique relationship with YHWH, the covenant-keeping God of Israel. He was the one, the eternal Son of the Father who fulfilled the covenant.[7]

> In the beginning was the Word and the Word was with God and the Word was God. He was in the beginning with God. All things came into being by him and apart from him nothing that came into being came into being. (John 1:1–2)

Yet we, like the Israelites of old, want to *see* God. If we are honest, we think that a glimpse of the "backside" of God, like the one Moses had (Exod. 33:23), would give us more confidence in God's reality, glory, and power. This was in fact the desire of the disciples. Philip said, "Lord, show us the Father and that will be enough for us." Jesus answered:

> "Don't you know me, Philip, even after I have been among you such a long time? *Anyone who has seen me has seen the Father.*

---

7. See "On the Road to Becoming Flesh: Israel as the Womb of the Incarnation in the Theology of T. F. Torrance" (http://perichoresis.org/downloads/IsraelastheWomboftheIncarnation.pdf).

How can you say, 'Show us the Father'? Don't you believe that
I am in the Father, and that the Father is in me? The words I
say to you are not just my own. Rather, it is the Father, living
in me, who is doing his work. Believe me when I say that I am
in the Father and the Father is in me; or at least believe on the
evidence of the miracles themselves. I tell you the truth, anyone
who has faith in me will do what I have been doing. He will
do even greater things than these, because I am going to the
Father." (John 14:9–12 NIV)

The four Gospels begin the narrative of Jesus at very different points.
Mark opens his Gospel with the ministry of John the Baptist, announcing the coming Messiah. Matthew begins with Jesus' ancestry, linking
him to Abraham (Jesus is a Jew, a son of David, a son of Abraham).
Luke traces Jesus' genealogy all the way back to Adam and ultimately
to God himself, saying that Adam (and thus all humanity after him)
was the Son of God. John says in effect that this is all true, but it is not
the whole truth because the narrative begins not with Abraham and not
even with Adam; it begins before creation.

In the Beginning Was the Word

John presents the beginning long before Genesis. In fact, if we want
to be technical, John's beginning is not a beginning—it is an eternal
reality. Before God does anything with reference to creation, he exists
in face-to-face relationship with His Word. As noted in the previous
chapter, John is a good Jew; he has learned Torah and he knows Genesis
1:1. "In the beginning God created the heavens and the earth." It is as if
John is saying, "That's true, but in the multicultural, pagan philosophical world I live in, 'God' is a very vague or ambiguous word. Everybody
believes in God or a god or the gods. The question is not 'Did God
create?' but 'Which God created?'" John says, in effect, "We're going to
get this from the very beginning. I'm not going to let anybody off the
hook: Jews, Greeks, even the church. 'In the beginning was the Word,
and the Word was with God, and the Word was God' (1:1)."

In John 1, if we look down to verse 18 we come back to the idea
presented in verse 1. Exegetes call this a "sandwich construction," or
an *inclusio*, where the same idea is used at the beginning and the end of

the section to bracket what is said in between. The intervening material fleshes out the repeated main idea. Because this passage is so familiar to us, we do not recognize the earth-shattering implications of what John is saying! He is challenging the Jews and pagans as well as the church (which as yet did not have a *doctrine* of the Trinity). Certainly both the Jews and the pagans did not accept the fact that Jesus had existed eternally in a face-to-face relationship with the Father. But at the time that John was writing, even his Christian audience did not fully grasp this reality or its implications. The Gentiles scoffed at the idea that the transcendent unknowable God could become man. The Jews, as well, rejected this idea out of hand. And as we saw in the previous chapter, the early church had some inkling that Jesus was God, but John is insisting that it is Jesus in himself who has explained or revealed who God is in himself—and that is mind-boggling![8] Notice verse 18: "No one has seen God at any time. The only-begotten God [or Son] who is in the bosom of the Father, he has explained him." The point here is that "In the beginning was the Word and the Word was with God" (i.e., in face-to-face relationship from eternity) and that this Word is the one who is "in the bosom of the Father" (i.e., in intimate closeness of relationship).[9]

John's phraseology in verse 1, "the Word was with God," doesn't allow for the interpretation that this Word was simply *a god,* as the Jehovah's Witnesses claim.[10] The Word is in a face-to-face relationship, that is, in a position of equality with God (the Father). In the division between what is God and what he is not, this means that this Word is on the same side of the divide, equal to and identified with God and as God. *All* that God

---

8. The word John uses here is the word normally translated "exegete," which literally means to "lead out" the meaning.

9. The translator's note in the New English Translation says of the literal Greek "in the bosom of": "an idiom for closeness or nearness; cf. Louw and Nida, *Greek-English Lexicon of the New Testament Based on Semantic Domains,* 34.18; BDAG 556 s.v. κόλπος" (Bauer, Arndt, Gingrich, and Danker, eds., 3rd ed., *A Greek-English Lexicon of the New Testament and Other Early Christian Literature* [Chicago: University of Chicago Press, 2001]). Its rendering of the second part of verse 18 is "The only one, himself God, who is in closest fellowship with the Father, has made God known."

10. With reference to the grammar of this phrase the translator's note in the NET Bible states:

Colwell's Rule is often invoked to support the translation of θεός (*theos*) as definite ("God") rather than indefinite ("a god") here. However, Colwell's Rule merely *permits,* but does not demand, that a predicate nominative ahead of an equative verb

is, the Word is. John is going far beyond the *Shema*: this is not just "Hear, O Israel, the LORD our God the LORD is one!" (Deut. 6:4 NASB). John *appears* to be saying at this point that there are two Gods. This is not where he ends of course, for a great deal of the material from which the doctrine of the Trinity developed is given by John in his Gospel.

Is God Really Like Jesus?

When we think of Jesus, we typically think of the baby who was born in Bethlehem more than two thousand years ago, who grew up and walked that narrow band of the earth that is Israel, teaching, healing, and announcing the kingdom. We think of his death and his resurrection, and we may even think of his ascension. We may say that we believe that Jesus is God, but we don't really *apprehend* let alone *comprehend* the indescribable unity between the Father and the Son (and the Spirit). Many of us, affirming that Jesus is God, believe at the same time that Jesus and the Father are different: while Jesus may be all for us, the Father has to be appeased in order to put up with us. If we are honest, many of us are afraid of the Father. We are afraid that if we mess up we

---

be translated as definite rather than indefinite. Furthermore, Colwell's Rule did not deal with a third possibility, that the anarthrous predicate noun may have more of a qualitative nuance when placed ahead of the verb. A definite meaning for the term is reflected in the traditional rendering "the word was God." From a technical standpoint, though, it is preferable to see a qualitative aspect to anarthrous θεός in John 1:1c. (See Daniel B. Wallace, *Greek Grammar Beyond the Basics: An Exegetical Syntax of the New Testament* [Grand Rapids: Zondervan, 1996], 266–69). Translations like the NEB, REB, and Moffatt are helpful in capturing the sense in John 1:1c, that the Word was fully deity in essence (just as much God as God the Father). However, in contemporary English "the Word was divine" (Moffatt) does not quite catch the meaning since "divine" as a descriptive term is not used in contemporary English exclusively of God. The translation "what God was the Word was" is perhaps the most nuanced rendering, conveying that everything God was in essence, the Word was too. This points to unity of essence between the Father and the Son without equating the persons. However, in surveying a number of native speakers of English, some of whom had formal theological training and some of whom did not, the editors concluded that the fine distinctions indicated by "what God was the Word was" would not be understood by many contemporary readers. Thus the translation "the Word was fully God" was chosen because it is more likely to convey the meaning to the average English reader that the Logos (which "became flesh and took up residence among us" in John 1:14 and is thereafter identified in the Fourth Gospel as Jesus) is one in essence with God the Father. The previous phrase, "the Word was with God," shows that the Logos is distinct in person from God the Father.

will be kicked out, or at least sent to our room for an indefinite "time out"; we are afraid that the Father brings punishment and retribution on us if we screw up, so we had better keep our ducks in a row. In short, at a visceral level, we believe that God is the judge and policeman whom we can never please and from whom we must be protected or rescued by Jesus. As a result, most of us live with some level of fear of the Father.

> No one has ever seen God. The only one, himself God, who is in closest fellowship with the Father, has made God known. (John 1:18)

But the apostle John says that the Son who is "in the bosom of the Father," in intimate fellowship with him, has explained him; and quotes Jesus as saying, "Whoever has seen me has seen the Father." Thomas Torrance speaks powerfully to an issue that plagues many believers. Is there a sort of wedge between God and Jesus? He says that we are dealing here

> with a theological principle which is of immense importance in pastoral care. How often people have said to me: "Will God really turn out to be what we believe him to be in Jesus Christ?" That is a question I have been asked on the battlefield by a young man who had barely half an hour to live: "Is God really like Jesus?" Questions like that which gnaw at the back of people's minds but which they suppress and which come to the surface only in moments of sharp crisis and hurt, tell us of the insidious damage done to people's faith by dualist habits of thought which drive a wedge between Jesus and God. Fearful anxiety arises in the human heart when people cannot connect Jesus up in their faith or understanding with the ultimate Being of God, for then the ultimate Being of God can be to them only dark, harsh angry streaks upon his face. It is quite different when the face of Jesus is identical with the face of God, when his forgiveness of sin is forgiveness indeed for its promise is made good through the atoning sacrifice of God in Jesus Christ, and when

the perfect love of God embodied in him casts out all fear. But all that depends upon the identity between Christ's mediation of divine revelation and reconciliation and his own Personal Being as *Mediator*.[11]

In short, there is no wedge between Jesus and the Father. There is no dark side of God. To know Jesus *is* to know the Father.

We will begin, then, with the creation of the world, and with God its Maker. For the first fact that you must grasp is this: the renewal of creation has been wrought by the Self-same Word who made it in the beginning. There is thus no inconsistency between creation and salvation; for the One Father has employed the same Agent for both works, effecting the salvation of the world through the same Word Who made it in the beginning.
—ATHANASIUS, *On the Incarnation*, 1:1[12]

Jesus: The Creator of All

In the previous chapter I spoke at some length about Jesus being the agent of creation. I do not want to belabor the fact of creation here. I just mention again the passages in the New Testament that speak of Jesus as the agent of creation. It is by, through, and for him.

- In the beginning was the Word, and the Word was with God, and the Word was fully God. The Word was with God in the beginning. *All things were created by him, and apart from him not one thing was created that has been created.* (John 1: 1–3)
- He is the image of the invisible God, the firstborn over all creation, *for all things in heaven and on earth were created by him—all*

---

11. Thomas F. Torrance, *The Mediation of Christ* (Colorado Springs, CO: Helmers & Howard, 1992), 59–60.

12. Athanasius, *On the Incarnation* (n.p.: CCEL.org, n.d.), 1:1.

> *things, whether visible or invisible, whether thrones or dominions, whether principalities or powers—all things were created through him and for him.* He himself is before all things and all things are held together in him. (Col. 1:15–17)

- After God spoke long ago in various portions and in various ways to our ancestors through the prophets, in these last days he has spoken to us in a son, whom he appointed heir of all things, and *through whom he created the world.* The Son is the radiance of his glory and the representation of his essence, and he sustains all things by his powerful word. (Heb. 1:1)

The ancient Greeks presupposed that matter was eternal. The unnamed and unknown god who made the world was not so much a creator as a designer, engineer, and artificer. The title used for him is "demiurge." Some have argued that Genesis 1 viewed against the background of the ancient Near Eastern religions is somewhat ambiguous in that the text allows for the creation account to be understood as a designing and producing of the earth out of pre-existing "stuff."[13] While I don't want to argue this point here, it is abundantly clear that the book of Hebrews unambiguously declares what we would describe as *creatio ex nihilo*, creation out of nothing.[14]

By faith we understand that the worlds were framed by the Word of God, so that the things which we see now did not come into being out of things which had previously appeared. (Heb. 11:3)

This truth is unpacked by the early church fathers. For example, Athanasius states:

---

13. See Bruce K. Waltke, *Creation and Chaos* (Portland: Western Seminary, 1975). This lecture series was serialized in *Bibliotheca Sacra* in 1975.

14. See the Wikipedia article "Ex nihilo" (http://en.wikipedia.org/wiki/Ex_nihilo) for a further discussion of the concept of *ex nihilo*.

For God is good—or rather, of all goodness He is Fountainhead, and it is impossible for one who is good to be mean or grudging about anything. Grudging existence to none therefore, He made all things out of nothing through His own Word, our Lord Jesus Christ; and of all these His earthly creatures He reserved especial mercy for the race of men. Upon them, therefore, upon men who, as animals, were essentially impermanent, He bestowed a grace which other creatures lacked—namely, the impress of His own Image, a share in the reasonable being of the very Word Himself, so that, reflecting Him and themselves becoming reasonable and expressing the Mind of God even as He does, though in limited degree, they might continue forever in the blessed and only true life of the saints in paradise.[15]

Jesus: The Sustainer of Creation

Christians believe that God created the universe *ex nihilo* (even if they do not recognize that the pre-incarnate Son was the agent of creation; failure to recognize this fact has led to a host of other theological errors, but these are beyond the scope of this discussion). What we Western Christians often forget, however—living as we do in the shadow of the Enlightenment and therefore thinking of the creation as a solid, independently existing thing—is that the New Testament also unambiguously testifies that Jesus is the one who *continually upholds* the creation. Creation has no existence independent of the active intimate ongoing work of God through Jesus. To ignore this is to live as practical deists, as if the universe were a closed system from which God has excluded himself.

Deism asserted that God brought creation into existence at the beginning. He created the universe to operate on its own self-sustaining principles expressed in natural law. He then withdrew his active presence and left creation to run on its own. Because of this the deists denied miracles generally, and hence specifically the incarnation.[16]

---

15. Athanasius, *On the Incarnation*, 1:3 (http://www.worldinvisible.com/library/athanasius/incarnation/incarnation.1.htm).

16. Deism ultimately had its roots in the work of Sir Isaac Newton. Newton was a devout religious individual who adopted a theological position similar to that of Arius, the fourth-century opponent of Athanasius. As noted previously, Arius had

Deism sank its roots deep into the psyche of Western culture. During the seventeenth century in England a group of scholars and theologians sought to defend historic Christianity from the onslaught of deism with its denial of the Trinity. One great irony of this defense was that within seventy-five years of that initial clash with deism, the intellectual descendants of those initial defenders of historic Christianity had adopted an understanding of God's ongoing relationship to the world that was virtually indistinguishable from that of the deists—the universe was a clockwork. The significant exception was that the orthodox still allowed room for God to break into the system from the outside to perform occasional miracles.[17]

Contemporary Bible-believing Christians, who are the intellectual heirs of those discussions, are in many ways practical deists. By default, our view of the nature of the cosmos is virtually indistinguishable from those who are deists (or even atheists). Like the deists we see God as creator, and conceive of creation as operating independently according to natural law. God is uninvolved with the day-to-day operations of the world. But this is not a biblical position. We find in the Old Testament that God is intimately involved in the ongoing happenings in the created order. Whether these ongoing happenings have to do with earthquakes and pestilence, or rain and sunshine, YHWH, the covenant-keeping God of Israel in his role as *Elohim*, the creator and ruler of creation, is intimately involved in all.

The New Testament opens up an even more profound truth to us. We find that it is not just God who is involved in creation. It is specifically *Jesus Christ, the beloved Son of the Father, who is both the creator and sustainer of all material and spiritual reality.* The New Testament witnesses to this reality over and over again.

---

insisted that God was singular and indivisible, and hence could not be Trinity. The Word spoken of by the apostle John was not himself God, but rather the first creation by God, who in turn created the natural order. The problem with this is that the pre-incarnate Christ is a creature who has "nothing proper to do with God." The Word was, in short, a demigod—powerful, yet himself created by the one eternal God. Athanasius understood that if Arius's claim were to take hold, the possibility of salvation would be destroyed.

17. For more on this, see Ian G. Barbour, *Issues in Science and Religion* (Englewood Cliffs, NJ: Prentice-Hall, 1966), 37–55, esp. 37–40.

We non-scientists still inhabit the Newtonian clockwork universe, implicitly denying the day-to-day involvement of God in the created order. But those working in the hard sciences proclaim that the Newtonian universe has been superseded. The reality we now inhabit is one described by Albert Einstein on the one hand and the work of quantum physicists on the other. We now understand that reality is not made up of independently self-existing individual pieces. Rather, *the cosmos is dynamic and interconnected at a quantum level.* And it is an open system—not a closed, mechanistic one! The significance of this paradigm shift is that, from a scientific perspective, there is no reason to deny the direct and immediate work of God within the system—including miracles.[18] Friends of mine who are physicists tell me that, whether on the macro level of the Big Bang or the micro level of quantum physics, the deeper researchers delve into these processes the more questions of God arise in their minds. So overpowering is this reality that numerous quantum physicists, having witnessed the interconnectedness of everything on a quantum level, have embraced what could be called "quantum spirituality," which easily slips into pantheism.

What or who is the logic behind the origin and the continuation of the universe? It is the Word, God the Son, who is also a man, Jesus, the Messiah. It is through his creativity, generosity, love, and goodness that there is *something* rather than nothing. It is because of his love, goodness, and faithfulness that we and our world continue to exist today.

The scientific method, while tremendously useful, has hard limits. Exclusively materialistic in its orientation, it cannot account for love or purpose or goodness or beauty. It can describe questions of *what* and *how* on a physical level, but cannot address issues of *who* or *why*.

As I have written elsewhere, theological understanding of God must be more, not less than scientific:

> Our theology should have not only a functional structure but also a beauty and attractiveness that reflect the beauty of God, who is himself the source of beauty. Astrophysicists who are searching for a "unified field theory" that will explain and unify

18. See the work of Giuseppe Del Re, *The Cosmic Dance: Science Discovers the Mysterious Harmony of the Universe* (Radner, PA: Templeton Foundation, 2000).

our knowledge of how the universe came into being and how the fundamental forces of nature are related speak of the "beauty principle." They have discovered in their advancing knowledge significant new insights that have an "elegant simplicity" about them. It is this very elegance that is a compelling feature in the acceptance of the new theory. Likewise, our theology should have a compelling beauty about it. If it does not, we probably need to do more reflection to grasp more fully who God is and what he has done.[19]

The psalmist speaks of the glory of God in the heavens (Psalm 19). The apostle Paul testifies of God's goodness that he freely pours out on all humanity and declares that he is not far from us (Acts 17:27). The presence of beauty in creation, whether it be seen in the magnificent images of the distant galaxies and nebulae, in a purple, orange, and pink sunset, in the unique bloom of a single rose, or even the most ephemeral thing—the playfulness of a breeze—is witness to the fact that God is "not a God who doesn't care, who lives away up there." Jesus is never far from us. His handiwork surrounds us in beauty and subtlety. His creativity and artwork speaks for itself. He is not so insecure that he has to sign the lower corner of a magnificent sunset: "made by Jesus."

The Anointed One

In this section I have purposely avoided use of the term "Messiah" (Hebrew) or "Christ" (Greek translation of the Hebrew) because the popular perception of these terms misses a central point of the meaning. For us twenty first-century Westerners, the title "Christ" has been reduced to little more than Jesus' surname, or at best regarded as his "divine" name in contrast to his "human" name "Jesus." Likewise the term "Messiah" has largely lost touch with its original meaning, "anointed one." Instead, "Messiah" is usually understood to refer to a political or spiritual deliverer who would rescue Israel from its oppressors. While this is true, it misses the meaning of the term "anoint."

---

19. M. James Sawyer, *The Survivor's Guide to Theology* (Grand Rapids: Zondervan, 2006), 19.

Luke's quotation of Isaiah is in the larger context of the baptism of Jesus.[20] He was the man who, alone of all men who ever lived, received the Holy Spirit without measure and permanently, and who through the baptism of the Holy Spirit was in constant communion with his Father.

> The Spirit of the Lord is upon me, because he has anointed me to proclaim good news to the poor. He has sent me to proclaim release to the captives and the regaining of sight to the blind, to set free those who are oppressed, to proclaim the year of the Lord's favor. (Luke 4:18–19)

Jesus was indeed the Anointed One, the Messiah, but not the Messiah expected by the Jews. The Jews in the first century had poured all their hopes and aspirations into the promised Anointed One. Many saw the foretold deliverance as a deliverance from Gentile domination, with a political inversion that would place Israel on top to dominate the Gentile powers. In reality, the foretold deliverance referred to something far greater than the Jews could begin to imagine: rescue from the fallenness of the creation that had plagued humanity since Adam and Eve. The conquest to be accomplished by the Anointed One was radical. By a breathtaking, bold, and counterintuitive plan it would bring life out of death, and reconciliation out of hatred and fear. The essence of Jesus' messianic mission can be expressed in the phrase "to set free."[21]

The Messiah's conquest was "good news" of the most unexpected kind. The translators of the King James Version used the term "gospel" to translate the Greek term *euanggelion*. In the early seventeenth century, "gospel" was not a technical religious/Christian term. It was an ordinary secular term used regularly to refer (in the words of sixteenth-century English reformer and translator William Tyndale) to the kind of

---

20. In the previous chapter Luke relates the descent of the Holy Spirit in the form of a dove who remained on Jesus.

21. Understood in the sense that he breaks the enslaving powers of sin and ushers

"good, glad, merry news that makes a man fairly leap for joy!" In a very real sense, Jesus is this "good, glad, merry news that makes a man fairly leap for joy!"[22] He himself is the gospel.

This means that the focus of the gospel is not what we normally think. We have inverted the gospel and made it about us—about human beings and how we can be saved. But from the New Testament perspective according to the apostle Paul, it is about Jesus and what he has done: "For I passed on to you as of first importance what I also received: that Christ died for our sins according to the Scriptures, and that he was buried, and that he was raised on the third day according to the Scriptures" (1 Cor. 15:3–4). As has been said, "The gospel is a declaration, not an invitation!" It is a declaration of Christ's cosmic lordship.[23]

N. T. Wright is right (no pun intended) in observing that in Paul's writings (and by extension in the New Testament as a whole), "the gospel"

> was not primarily a message about sinful human beings and how they attained justification and salvation . . . If we are to understand and appropriate Paul we will do well to use his words in his way. For him, "the gospel" was the sovereign message, from none other than God, concerning Jesus the Messiah, God's unique son. This message was not simply the offer of a new reordering of one's private spiritual interiority, a new clearing up of a morally dysfunctional life via forgiveness for the

---

in the age of the freedom of the Spirit associated with Jesus's cosmic Lordship (Phil. 2:6–11).

22. The point here is not that we are to read the medieval understanding of gospel back into the Greek *euangelion*, but that the translators of the King James Version saw this non-technical English term as best expressing the sense of the Greek term. *BDAG* (acronym for Bauer, Danker, Arndt, and Gingrich, editors of *A Greek-English Lexicon of the New Testament and Other Early Christian Literature*, published by University of Chicago Press; 3rd ed. in 2001) defines the term as occurring "in our lit. only in the sense of good news relating to God's action in Jesus Christ." While we usually divide our studies of Jesus into his person on the one hand and his work on the other, this is an artificial distinction that conceptually divides who he is from what he has done. Apart from his identity as the eternal Son of the Father, Jesus's work has no redemptive or cosmic significance.

23. See Philippians 2:6–11.

past and new moral energy for the present. It was not simply a
new vocation to live for God and for others in the world. It was
rather, news about God and about Jesus; news that this Jesus
had become the spearhead of God's "age to come"; news that,
within this age the principalities and powers, including earthly
rulers, the powers of darkness, and sin and death themselves
had been defeated and were now summoned to allegiance. "The
gospel" was a command requiring obedience, much more than
an invitation seeking a response.[24]

When we sing the "Hallelujah Chorus" at Christmastime we may declare an expectation or hope that Christ will return to establish his
kingdom—but the gospel speaks of an accomplished fact! He has already been crowned Lord of all! He has yet to return and take possession of his earthly kingdom. This is not to deny the need for us to
recognize and believe the reality that Christ is cosmic Lord by whose
crucifixion and resurrection alienated humanity and creation have been
reconciled to God. The issue of human response to the gospel attends
the gospel, but it is not the gospel itself.[25]

One of Us

My wife confessed that when she first heard the song "One of Us,"
written by Eric Bazilian and popularized by Joan Osborne, her reaction
was something between being offended and being appalled. It sounded
somehow irreverent if not outright blasphemous. Yet however shocking
it seems, because of the incarnation God *has* become one of us. He
looked like a common slob just like us. I have no discomfort in saying
this because Jesus was born in a stable, with its fragrant (?) aroma. (I
grew up on a farm and have shoveled literally tons of cow manure—I
know the smell well. There is nothing quaint or romantic about it; it
stinks.) He grew up poor. He worked as a carpenter. When he preached

---

24. N. T. Wright, "The Letter to the Romans," in *The New Interpreter's Bible*, vol.
10 (Nashville: Abingdon, 2002), 427.

25. With reference to the content of the message, see J. I. Packer, *Evangelism and
the Sovereignty of God* (Downers Grove, IL: InterVarsity Press, 2008), 49–52.

his needs were supplied by friends and followers, and when he died he possessed only the clothes on his back.

What if God was one of us? Just a slob like one of us[26]

But we are uncomfortable with the full humanity of God in Christ. Since the early medieval period we Western Christians have believed that Christ's humanity was special and different from our own: it was miraculously unfallen. To buttress this understanding the Catholic Church teaches the immaculate conception of Mary, that she was born without the stain of original sin so she could bear one who was without the stain of original sin. Jesus was thus qualified to be the perfect sacrifice, and his perfection consisted not only in committing no personal sin, but in being unstained by original sin.

But this is a misunderstanding of the work of God. The problem with Adamic humanity is not simply or primarily acts of sin, however horrendous and guilt-producing those acts may be. While the focus of the Old Testament was sins, the focus of the New Testament is radically different: the condition of the heart. We sin because of the twisted, alienated condition of our hearts. In theological language we say we are fallen, depraved. Judicial forgiveness of sins, *as vital as it is,* cannot alter this heart condition. The problem, and therefore the solution, is not only, or even primarily, judicial. It is ontological: it involves more than our legal status, *it involves our very being.* What is needed is *healing.* The ancient church understood this.[27] *A Jesus who is ontologically separate from our broken, fallen humanity is unable to change its very nature from the inside.* This is a radical notion that needs considerable expansion; we will spend the next few sections of this chapter on it.

---

26. Eric Bazilian, "One of Us," recorded by Joan Osborne (Universal Music Publishing Group, Warner/Chappell Music, Inc., EMI Music Publishing, 1995).

27. For an excellent summary of the Nicene understanding of the humanity of Christ, see Thomas F. Torrance, *The Christian Frame of Mind* (Colorado Springs, CO: Helmers & Howard, 1989), 1–16.

Within fundamentalism and evangelicalism as well as historic Protestantism, the atonement is understood as a legal transaction, summed up in the concept of the *vicarious death* of Christ. (I discuss the important and related though often ignored concept, *the vicarious humanity* of Christ, in more detail at the end of this chapter.) Christ suffered in our place and for us on the cross so we would not suffer eternally. This account of the atonement, called "penal substitution," was first articulated as a comprehensive explanation of the nature of the atonement during the Reformation. Ultimately, it arises out of a conceptual matrix of law and justice that has its roots in Roman jurisprudence rather than in Scripture. All of Western theology has been affected by the forensic cast of Roman law since the third-century work of Tertullian, a brilliant Roman lawyer.

Beginning with this understanding of the necessity of the perfect sacrifice, the significance of Christ's humanity was reduced to the fact that he was born without any stain of fallenness and led a sinless life, which qualified him as the perfect sacrifice. Additionally, his deity gave his death infinite worth so as to pay for the sin(s) of all humanity. While this is mostly true, it badly misses the larger point! The goal of the incarnation is not only the provision of forgiveness, it is *adoption*: the establishment of a personally intimate relationship with the triune God—a theme articulated in the New Testament nearly as often as justification, but virtually ignored by the church.[28] Significantly, the leading patristic fathers, Irenaeus, Athanasius, Cyril of Alexandria, and Augustine, recognized that salvation was not to be thought of simply as forgiveness, or even justification (i.e., right standing or a judicial declaration of "not guilty" because of the imputation of Christ's righteousness to our account); rather, "in salvation we receive the Logos (God

---

28. Douglas Fairbairn discusses the idea of adoption at length in relationship to the patristic concept of *theosis* (often referred to as deification) as part of the relational blessing of sonship that believers enjoy. *Theosis*, which includes both adoption and participation in the *koinonia*, or fellowship, of the Father and the Son, was the central feature of the patristic understanding of salvation: "[F]orgiveness and becoming Christlike flow from our participation in a relationship, from our becoming sons by adoption so as to share in the communion that the natural Son has with God the Father" (Douglas Fairbairn, *Life in the Trinity: An Introduction to Theology with the Help of the Church Fathers* [Downers Grove, IL: InterVarsity Press, 2009], loc. 407, Kindle ed.).

the Son) himself. We do not receive something he gives us, because the Son gives us his very self. And the essence of this gift of himself is that we become sons and daughters of God. We are adopted into the same relationship he has with God."[29] Even the Reformer John Calvin recognized that the reality of union with Christ (being *in Christ*) is more foundational than justification by faith![30] As Paul says in Ephesians 1:4–5: "He chose us in Christ before the foundation of the world that we may be holy and unblemished in his sight in love. He did this by *predestining us to adoption as his sons* through Jesus Christ according to the pleasure of his will" (my emphasis). The image of adoption moves the focus from our legal courtroom status to our status as *beloved children within the family*.

While on the cross Christ fulfilled his role as the atoning sacrifice, we do not realize that his whole life was in a larger sense part of the atonement (at-one-ment), as Calvin said. From the moment of his birth, he was doing more than preparing for death by leading a perfect life; he was paying the price of our liberation *by living our life for us*.[31] His whole life was a harrowing ordeal of struggle, of suffering, of trial and tribulation and pain, as he penetrated deeper and deeper into human estrangement from God and neighbor. On the cross he experienced to the fullest extent the darkness, hopelessness, and helplessness of Adamic estrangement from the Father—he is fully immersed in the depths of

---

29. Ibid., loc. 784–95, Kindle ed.

30. Alister E. McGrath, *Reformation Thought: An Introduction*, 3rd ed. (Oxford: Blackwell, 1999), 125.

31. John Calvin, *Institutes of the Christian Religion*, trans. Ford Lewis Battles (Philadelphia: Westminster, 1977), 2.16.5: "Now someone asks, How has Christ abolished sin, banished the separation between us and God, and acquired righteousness to render God favorable and kindly toward us? To this we can in general reply that he has achieved this for us by the whole course of his obedience. This is proved by Paul's testimony: 'As by one man's disobedience many were made sinners, so by one man's obedience we are made righteous' [Rom. 5:19]. In another passage, to be sure, Paul extends the basis of the pardon that frees us from the curse of the law to the whole life of Christ: 'But when the fullness of time came, God sent forth his Son, born of woman, subject to the law, to redeem those who were under the law' [Gal. 4:4–5]. Thus in his very baptism, also, he asserted that he fulfilled a part of righteousness in obediently carrying out his Father's commandment [Matt. 3:15]. In short, from the time when he took on the form of a servant, he began to pay the price of liberation in order to redeem us."

Adamic humanity and for the first time experiences personally the full extent of our darkness, estrangement, and alienation.

And for this reason it was that He graciously poured Himself out, that He might gather us into the bosom of the Father. [32]
—IRENAEUS, *Against the Heresies*, V.2.1

Jesus cries out in anguish, "My God, my God, why have you forsaken me?" To be emphatic here: the Father did not turn his back on the Son; he did not turn his face away "because he could not look on sin." No matter how widely held such notions are, they are utter foolishness if not outright blasphemous, and reveal a profound ignorance of the nature of God as Trinity. That the Father could turn his back on the Son is a theological impossibility—the unity of the Trinity utterly forbids such a conclusion. The Father was there, Jesus was still the Anointed One, anointed with the Spirit without measure.[33] In fact, Scripture states explicitly that Jesus offered himself up through the eternal Spirit.[34] Here Jesus, as the Father's beloved Son, was echoing the language of Psalm 22:1—which, for any Jew who heard Jesus or read the Gospel account, would bring to mind the entire psalm and the experience of the psalmist. Jesus was using the psalm, interpreting for the witnesses what was

---

32. Alexander Roberts and James Donaldson (eds.), *The Ante-Nicene Fathers* I (New York: Charles Scribner's Sons, 1905), 527.

33. We must draw a vital distinction here between what we feel experientially and what is actually happening objectively. Saints throughout the ages have reported times, sometimes extended periods of time, when they could not *feel* the presence of God with them. Yet we have the explicit promise of Scripture that the Father will never leave or forsake us (Heb. 13:5). Jesus's experience on the cross was one of penetrating the depth of human alienation from God, experiencing the common human feeling of being totally lost and unfindable, even by God. While that is the experience, it does not reflect the reality of the situation. By penetrating the depth of human alienation Jesus can truly be said to understand and empathize with the most desperate expression of our hopelessness and helplessness.

34. Hebrews 9:14: "how much more will the blood of Christ, who through the eternal Spirit offered himself without blemish to God, purify our consciences from dead works to worship the living God."

happening before their eyes. Far from the Father turning his eyes away, the psalmist insists that just the opposite is true: "For he has not despised or abhorred the affliction of the afflicted; and *he has not hid his face from him*, but has heard, when he cried to him" (Ps. 22:24 RSV).[35] Amazingly, the psalm says exactly the opposite of what is regularly taught about Jesus' experience on the cross in relation to God and his holiness![36]

> The Word of God, who dwelt in man, and became the Son of Man, that He might accustom man to receive God, and God to dwell in man, according to the good pleasure of the Father.[37]
> —IRENAEUS, *Against the Heresies*, III.20.2

The mystery of Jesus is that he is fully God and fully man.[38] He did not just appear on the scene as a visible spirit to tell us what we could do to get to heaven. Those who adopted this teaching the apostle John labeled as Antichrist. The Son became a real flesh-and-blood human being from the fallen line of Adam (Luke 3). As Irenaeus affirmed in the late second century:

> Therefore, as I have already said, He caused man (human nature) to cleave to and to become one with God. For unless *man*

---

35. The translators' notes for the New English Translation indicate that the Hebrew phrase "hide one's face from" is actually an idiom meaning "ignore" (see Pss. 10:11; 13:1; 51:9). Sometimes the idiom carries the stronger meaning "reject" (see Pss. 27:9; 88:14).

36. See C. Baxter Kruger, *Jesus and the Undoing of Adam* (Jackson, MS: Perichoresis, 2001), 41–44, for a more detailed discussion of Psalm 22 and the following two Psalms 23 and 24, recognized for centuries as a messianic trilogy. See also Al Hsu's article, "He's Calling for Elijah! Why We Still Mishear Jesus," *Christianity Today* 56 (2012) (http://www.christianitytoday.com/ct/2012/aprilweb-only/my-god-forsaken-me.html?utm_source=ctdirect-html&utm_medium=eNews&utm_term=9482790&utm_content=123155853&utm_campaign=2012).

37. Ibid, 450.

38. See note 52 below for a brief discussion of the nature of Jesus's humanity.

had overcome the enemy of man, the enemy would not have been legitimately vanquished. And again: unless it had been *God* who had freely given salvation, we could never have possessed it securely. And unless *man* had been joined to *God*, he could never have become a partaker of incorruptibility. For it was incumbent upon the Mediator between God and men, by His relationship to both, to bring both into friendship and concord, and present man to God, while He revealed God to man. For, in what way, could we be partakers of the adoption of sons, unless we had received from Him through the Son that fellowship, which refers to Himself, unless His Word, having been made flesh, had entered into communion with us? Wherefore also He passed through every stage of life, restoring to all communion with God.[39]

Jesus is the concrete proof of God's love for us. More than this, he is the concrete demonstration of the humility of God. God, as Trinity, is humble, and loves his fallen creation—loves it enough to join in solidarity with us, the fallen crown of that creation. God, as man, lived life in the same circumstances and condition as the rest of us. He felt the fear, the angst, and the pain that we all feel. He felt the rejection, the condemnation, the disgust, the hatred, and all the other negative emotions and temptations that we feel, and with at least the same intensity. His deity did not shield him from anything; if anything, it intensified the experience. We misunderstand the point of the incarnation if we see Jesus merely as an instrument of God to pay for our sins. His entry into fallen Adamic existence is not just to be the perfect sacrifice; it is to convert and redeem humanity by absorbing the full consequences of our sin in life and in death, all the while living and dying as the one faithful human being in our humanity, and so to bring healing to the fear and alienation. God as Father, Son, and Spirit refused to let humanity continue in its helpless and hopeless condition. If he did not enter into the depth of our alienation and defy it by nevertheless continuing to love and obey God with his whole self, his blessings could not reach us. God's covenant between himself and Israel would go unfulfilled, and

---

39. Irenaeus, *Against Heresies, Ante-Nicene Fathers I*, 449. Italics added.

humanity would remain in thrall to the power of the evil one, unable to escape.[40]

The paradox at the heart of Christianity is that the Son of God entered into fallen Adamic existence without ceasing to be the Son of God. He became Adam without ceasing to be the faithful Son of the Father. The life of the Trinity intersected the brokenness of fallen human existence. How is this possible? How could the fellowship of the Trinity penetrate Adam's hiding? How could the togetherness and integrity of the Father, Son and Spirit enter into the brokenness and perversion of fallen Adamic existence? How could the one who knows the Father and loves Him with all of his heart enter into the wrongheadedness and blindness and projections of Adam and of Israel? How could this contradiction be possible?

The answer is that it is not possible—something has to give, something has to change. Either the fellowship of the Father, Son and Spirit grinds to an eternal halt, or Adamic existence is fundamentally reordered. Either the love of the Triune God is broken, or Adamic flesh is converted to God. There has to be a conversion, a fundamental restructuring either in the being and character of God, or in the being and character of Adam.

The entrance of the fellowship of the Father, Son and Spirit into our alienation and estrangement did not mean the ruin of the Trinity—it meant war. As Luke tells us, Jesus Christ beat his way forward by blows. The Son of God entered into our broken, fallen, alienated human existence. He took upon himself our fallen flesh. He stood in Adam's shoes, in Israel's shoes, in our shoes, and he steadfastly refused to be like Adam. He refused to be like Israel. He entered into fallen human existence and steadfastly refused to be "fallen" in it. Step by step, blow by blow, moment by moment, he refused to believe in the god of Adam and he loved his Father with all of his heart, soul, mind, and strength. Step by step, blow by blow, moment by moment, he hammered out his sonship on the anvil of fallen Adamic

---

40. Kruger, *Jesus and the Undoing of Adam*, 24.

existence. Step by step, blow by blow, moment by moment, he bent back the thoroughgoing wrongheadedness of the Adamic mind.[41]

The miracle and paradox of Jesus as the Anointed One was that although he was eternal God, he was born into our common estrangement and alienation, and shared the alienation of mind that we experience. As Calvin stated: "By his birth he was made like us in all respects [Heb. 2:17] that he might learn to feel our pain [cf. Heb. 5:2]."[42]

> [In] Frederick Buechner's description of compassion as "the sometimes fatal capacity for feeling what it's like to live in some-body else's skin. It is the knowledge that there can never really be any peace and joy for me until there is peace and joy finally for you too," I could only hear Jesus speaking to us all. For he is the only one who has suffered the fatal capacity of feeling what it is like to live in somebody else's skin. And he did so because he committed himself to us before the foundation of the world, and he will not rest until we too feel his peace and joy, and until the cosmos is expressing his own relationship with [the Father] and the Holy Spirit.[43]

God and fallen humanity come together in a single unified person, who nonetheless lived in perfect fellowship and unity with the Father; if he succumbed to temptation and broke the unity with the Father, all

---

41. Ibid., 25–26. Luke uses the term *prokoptō* to speak of Jesus growing in favor with God and man. While there is some debate as to the origin of the word, it was probably first used either as a nautical term meaning "to make headway in spite of blows," or, given its derivation, to refer to the work of a smith, who "with the blow" of his hammer "lengthens out" iron (G. Kittel, ed., *Theological Dictionary of the New Testament* [Grand Rapids: Eerdmans, 1968], 6:703). Kruger, following James B. Torrance, sees the term coming from the use of the forge and thus providing a vivid metaphor for sanctifying the Adamic flesh Jesus inherited, bending it back to its original condition throughout his life.

42. Calvin, *Institutes of The Christian Religion* (Philadelphia: Westminster, 1960), 2:16:19.

43. C. Baxter Kruger, *Baxter's Ongoing Thoughts*, 2009 (http://baxterkruger.blogspot.com/).

would be lost. The person of the God-man is an "impossible possibility." If God did not enter our alienation, he had nothing to give us—he could not rescue us. As Gregory of Nazianzus said in the fourth century, "That which he has not assumed he has not healed."[44] This became a key in the Nicene understanding of the person of Jesus. As the apostle John said so eloquently: "For this is the way God loved the world: he gave his one and only Son, so that everyone who believes in him will not perish but have eternal life. For God did not send his Son into the world to condemn the world, but that the world should be saved through him" (John 3:16–18).

> In Jesus Christ, God has shown not only *that he does not want to be God without us*, but that *he does not want us to be without him.* [45]
> —P. T. FORSYTH

> To put it in the simplest way, what unites God and us is that *He does not will to be God without us*, that He creates us rather to share with us and therefore with our being and life and act His own incomparable being life and act, that He does not allow His history to be His and ours, but causes them to take place as a common history.
> —KARL BARTH[46]

The humanity assumed by our Lord was the same humanity with the same weakness that we experience (Heb. 4:15). Unlike us he maintained his connection with the Father throughout his entire life and lived in dependence on the Spirit and in full communion with the Father.

---

44. Gregory of Nazianzus, "Letter 101 to Cledonius," in *Nicene and Post-Nicene Fathers Series, Second Series,* vol. 7, ed. Philip Schaff (Grand Rapids: Eerdmans, 1975), 441.

45. Quoted by Dave Cruver. *A Gospel Reflection on Love.* April 4, 2012, http://www.totellyouthetruth.net/?p=951

46. Karl Barth, *Church Dogmatics* IV, I (Edinburgh; T & T Clark, 1974), 7.

Excursus: The Wrath of God?

"The bow of God's wrath is bent, and the arrow
made ready on the string, and justice bends the
arrow at your heart, and strains the bow, and it is
nothing but the mere pleasure of God, and that of
an angry God, without any promise or obligation at
all, that keeps the arrow one moment from being
made drunk with your blood"[47]

—JONATHAN EDWARDS,
"Sinners in the Hands of an Angry God"

Jonathan Edwards's portrayal of the attitude of God in what is reputed to be the most famous sermon in American history by the
greatest thinker of Puritan New England reveals a jarring shift
from the attitude we see in Scripture and the early church concerning the Father's attitude toward fallen humanity. While it is true
that God hates sin, he loves the sinner—which is why he hates sin,
because of what it does to the sinner and the relationship. In the
epistles of Paul and John we nd that God has reconciled the world
to himself in Christ who is the "propitiation" or "expiation"[48] for

47. Jonathan Edwards "Sinners in the Hands of an Angry God." Preached July 8,
1741. http://www.ccel.org/ccel/edwards/sermons.1.html?highlight=sinners%20in%20
the%20hands%20of%20an%20angry%20god#highlight

48. The translation of the Greek is difficult, as is explained in the New English
Translation's note on 1 John 2:2:

A suitable English translation for this word (ἱλασμός, hilasmos) is a difficult and
even controversial problem. "Expiation," "propitiation," and "atonement" have all been
suggested. L. Morris, in a study that has become central to discussions of this topic
(*The Apostolic Preaching of the Cross*, 140), sees as an integral part of the meaning of
the word (as in the other words in the ἱλάσκομαι [hilaskomai] group) the idea of
turning away the divine wrath, suggesting that "propitiation" is the closest English
equivalent. It is certainly possible to see an averting of divine wrath in this context,
where the sins of believers are in view and Jesus is said to be acting as Advocate on
behalf of believers. R. E. Brown's point (*Epistles of John*, 220–21), that it is essentially
cleansing from sin which is in view here and in the other use of the word in 4:10, is
well taken, but the two connotations (averting wrath and cleansing) are not mutually

our sins as well as those of the whole world.[49] In fact, the first Bible verse that many of us learned as children is John 3:16: "For in this way God loved the world: he gave his one and only Son that everyone who believes in him should not perish but have eternal life."

A common popular conservative American evangelical articulation of the work of Christ is that the Son interposes himself between an angry God and rebellious humanity. Jesus becomes the divine whipping boy who absorbs God's anger at us. This caricature of the death of Christ instills fear into our hearts because it sows doubt about the Father's goodness and love for us. The reality is that while Jesus is our representative and mediator, and his death deals with our sin as well as sins, it is far more than just a legal payment for law-breaking. In addition to reducing the Father to judge, such a solution is external to us; while solving the problem of legal guilt, it would leave us personally and ontologically untouched. The much fuller picture is that *Adamic humanity itself* was crucified in the death of Jesus, and that in his resurrection he became the last Adam, the progenitor of *a new redeemed humanity into which we have been incorporated.*

While Edwards preached on the love of God ten times more than he preached on the anger of God and his outrage and hatred of sin *and the sinner,* simply believing that there is such a dark side to God is a hindrance to establishing a meaningful relationship with him. The early church, however, knew no such understanding. We find there a radically different conception of the attitude of God. Hear the words of Athanasius, the fourth-century Alexandrian bishop responsible for defending the eternal equality of the Father and the Son as expressed by the Nicene Creed:

---

exclusive and it is unlikely that the propitiatory aspect of Jesus' work should be ruled out entirely in the usage in 2:2. Nevertheless, the English word "propitiation" is too technical to communicate to many modern readers, and a term like "atoning sacrifice" (given by Webster's *New International Dictionary* as a definition of "propitiation") is more appropriate here. Another term, "satisfaction," might also convey the idea, but "satisfaction" in Roman Catholic theology is a technical term for the performance of the penance imposed by the priest on a penitent.

49. 2 Corinthians 5:19; 1 John 2:2.

It was unworthy of the goodness of God that creatures made by Him should be brought to nothing through the deceit wrought upon man by the devil; and it was supremely un-fitting that the work of God in mankind should disappear, either through their own negligence or through the deceit of evil spirits. As, then, the creatures whom He had created . . . were on the road to ruin, what then was God, being Good, to do? Was He to let corruption and death have their way with them? In that case, what was the use of having made them in the beginning? Surely it would have been better never to have been created at all than, having been created, to be neglected and perish; and, besides that, such indifference to the ruin of His own work before His very eyes would argue not goodness in God but limitation. . . . It was impossible, therefore, that God should leave man to be carried off by corruption, be-cause it would be unfitting and unworthy of Himself.[50]

Since my college days I have been a Tolkien fan, and particular-ly a fan of *The Lord of the Rings*; in fact, I have read that trilogy cover to cover eight times. So I was excited and hopeful at the announcement that the masterpiece, which some believe to be the most important work of fiction in the twentieth century, was being brought to the big screen. (I was also a bit wary since it is so diffi-cult to successfully translate novels onto the big screen.) When *The Fellowship of the Ring* was released, I was not disappointed. In the story, particularly in the confrontation with the Balrog, Gandalf functions as a Christ-figure. He faces the overwhelming power of evil and darkness and roars, "You shall not pass!" In the con-frontation the Balrog is defeated, but at the cost of Gandalf's own life. Gandalf, unbeknownst to his distraught companions at the time, is then restored to life. This is the vision of the early church fathers on the sacrifice of Christ: it was a conquest of sin, death, and Satan.[51]

---

50. Athanasius, *The Treatise De Incarnatione Verbi Dei*, trans. and ed. by a Religious of C. S. M. V. (London: A. R. Mowbray & Co. 1941), § 6.

51. I am not saying that this understanding is a fully adequate explanation of the

atonement, but that the common account of the atonement as penal substitution is a serious reduction. Thomas F. Torrance, in his posthumously published *Atonement*, expounds on the atonement in the terms and categories laid out in the Old and New Testaments. The manifold theories of the atonement throughout the history of the church have inevitably become reductionistic, leaving on the "cutting-room floor" key concepts that could not be forced through the matrix of various theologians. Likewise N. T. Wright has faulted penal substitution as inadequate for its narrow vision of dealing with sins: "we have allowed 'atonement' to be narrowed down to 'forgiving sins so people can go to heaven,' leaving unaddressed the (to us quite different) problem of 'evil' as an abstract thing. This is a dangerous mistake" (N.T. Wright, *How God Became King* [New York: HarperCollins, 2012], loc. 2565, Kindle ed.).

Torrance contends that our conceptualization of the atonement must begin with the concepts and categories of the Old Testament because New Testament atonement images and metaphors are drawn from the Old. Particularly important are the categories of *padah* and *kipper* ("redeem," "ransom") and *gaal/goel* ("redeem," "redeemer"). Thus atonement thinking must involve a dramatic element, a cultic-forensic element, and an ontological element. These are brought together in the threefold office of Christ. See Thomas F. Torrance, *Atonement* (Downers Grove, IL: InterVarsity Press, 2009), xiv–xv, 24–96. Elsewhere he observes:

> The cross is not only a revelation of the love of Christ but a revelation of the love of God. The cross is a window opened into the very heart of God. The fact that the Father did not spare his only Son but delivered him up for us all, as St Paul expressed it, tells us that in the sacrifice of Christ on the cross it was the Father as well as the Son who paid the cost of our salvation, so that through the blood of Christ the innermost nature of God the Father as holy love became revealed to us. However, we must also say that as the incarnate Son is of one and the same being as God the Father, so the atoning act perfected in the cross of Jesus Christ is grounded in the very being of the eternal God, that is, in the eternal being of the Holy Trinity.
>
> . . . God's activity is not separate from his being but inheres in his being: it is his being-in-act or his act-in-being, not something in addition to his being but his very being in action. Thus the Atonement is to be regarded as the act of God in his being and his being in his act. This is not to say, of course, that it was the Father who was crucified, for it was the Son in his distinction from the Father who died on the cross, but it is to say that the suffering of Christ on the cross was not just human, it was divine as well as human, and in fact is to be regarded as the suffering of God himself, that is, as the being of God in his redeeming act, and the passion of God in his very being as God. Likewise . . . this applies also to the act and being of God the Holy Spirit, although it was the Son and not the Holy Spirit who died on the cross. Thus we cannot but think of the Atonement as a threefold act grounded in and issuing from the triune being of God. While the Father, the Son and the Holy Spirit are personally distinct from one another, they are nevertheless of one and the same being with one another in God, and their acts interpenetrate one another in the indivisibility of the one Godhead (Thomas F. Torrance, *The Mediation of Christ*, 112–13).

C. S. Lewis picks up on this same theme of dying on behalf of another or others in *The Lion, The Witch and The Wardrobe* when Aslan gives himself in exchange for Edmund to rescue him from the clutches of the White Witch. She thinks she will attain final victory and secure her hold on Narnia by killing Aslan. But she only knows the "Deep Magic" operative from the dawn of time; she does not know the "Deeper Magic" from *before* the dawn of time that thwarts her plan.

When Christ assumed our full broken humanity and united it with the Trinity, he was not acting as an individual human, but as the representative of the whole human race—taking us all with him, as it were. The apostle Paul declares that just as all were constituted sinners by one man's (Adam's) transgression, in the same manner one man's (Jesus') righteous act (his life, death, and resurrection on our behalf) brought righteousness leading to life for all people (Rom. 5:16–18). Paul makes it clear that as our representative, Jesus became the founder of a new humanity. He boldly declares a stunning objective reality: "Consequently, just as condemnation for all people came through one transgression, so too through the one righteous act came righteousness leading to life for all people" (Rom. 5:18). A couple of verses later we find that the grace of God is greater than the sin of humanity (or of any single human).

> For it was for this end that the Word of God
> was made man, and He who was the Son of God
> became the Son of Man, that man, having been taken
> into the Word, and receiving the adoption, might
> become the Son of God.[52]
> —IRENAEUS, *AGAINST THE HERESIES*, III.19.1

Clearly, the Jesus that most of us have grown up with or been introduced to is far from the Jesus of cosmic proportions we find

---

52. A. Cleveland Cox ed., *The Ante-Nicene Fathers*, vol. 1, (Grand Rapids: Eerdmans, 1977), 449.

on the pages of Scripture and unpacked by the early church. The question becomes: how would our lives change if we would embrace this Jesus, this cosmic Christ, with his claims to universal lordship over all creation?

The Incarnation as an Act of Love

The incarnation *must* be viewed as an act of love. The triune God created out of a desire to extend his eternal fullness of love beyond the persons of the Trinity, to that which was not himself. He created, knowing full well the cost—knowing that the crown of his creation, those who bore his image, would rebel and bring ruin not only on themselves but on all their descendants and the rest of creation. When the fall took place, he immediately set in motion the plan[53] to undo the damage by *personally identifying himself* in his fullness with his creation, by becoming flesh in the person of Jesus. To put this more colloquially, "God chose to get his hands dirty to rescue his children and clean up the mess they had made." That is the testimony of the apostle John (John 3:16–18). This seemingly impossible joining of infinite and holy deity with fallen and finite humanity is a concrete demonstration of his love for us his estranged children.

This is not to be understood simply in the sense that God "decided to love." To understand the incarnation we must reverse our normal manner of thinking and understand love in terms of the incarnation rather than the incarnation in terms of love. As Thomas Torrance has said, "Christianity reverses all our values. For example it reverses our idea of fatherhood. When we know God as Father we must confess that we as such do not know what real fatherhood is! Our fatherhood which we know is only fatherhood so far as it is named after the Father God (Eph. 3:15), not vice versa."[54] In other words, as discussed in chapter 2, we intuitively project our relationship with our human father onto God. As we consider God, we tend to envision him as the image of our father,

---

53. This plan was of course not an unforeseen salvage job. Scripture makes it plain that Jesus was the Lamb slain from before the foundation of the world (1 Peter 1:18–20).

54. Thomas F. Torrance, *The Doctrine of Jesus Christ* (Eugene, OR: Wipf & Stock, 2002), 86.

but raised to the nth degree—with the same harshness, absence, distance, emotional unavailability, or whatever other weakness our father had. It is by our encounter with God the Father that our concept of true fatherhood is redefined.

In the same way, we know what love is by the love of God demonstrated to us in the incarnation. The incarnation is an act of unconditional love, in that God did not wait for man to repent and start seeking him, but gave himself to us while we were still in rebellion against him. God's love for us is not caused by anything in us. As the apostle says in 1 John, "We love him because he first loved us" (4:19). Our love is responsive; divine love is prior, outlandish, and totally an expression of grace.

Nineteenth-century liberal theology codified as one of its axioms "the infinite value of the human soul." The problem with this is that it subtly but really presupposes a reason *in us* for God's love of us. It has been rightly observed that such thinking is grounded in human pride, "as if he (the individual human) could help God to love him, as if he could deride God if He did not love him! . . . 'God has to love me; He will not finally condemn me; because He would not be love otherwise!' To talk like this is to not understand the love of God in the least."[55] To argue this way is to contend that God's love is caused by something outside himself. It is to say that he—his love, since he *is* love—is not spontaneous, overflowing, abundant, and gracious as he has revealed himself to be. God's love is entirely free from any obligation outside his own being.

To repeat, God does not love us because of our inherent worth. Love is not based on inherent value. Rather, the value of an object is based on the fact that it is loved.

As a child I had two teddy bears. One was a traditional brown teddy bear, and the other was a panda. I loved the brown teddy bear but had no special affection for the panda. I held and snuggled with that brown teddy bear until it wore out. In fact, I kept it around until I was an adult. Somewhere along the way the panda disappeared and I didn't even miss it. But had I lost that brown teddy bear that was worn threadbare and missing one of its eyes, I would've been devastated. Why did I love it? I loved it just because I loved it. Certainly the resale value of the panda

---

55. Ibid., 87.

would've exceeded that of the brown teddy bear, which was fit for the trashcan. Just as value in the created world is not inherent but always imputed, so that something is worth whatever someone is willing to give for it, so it is with God and his valuing of us.

Just a couple more observations on the incarnation as an act of love, and what this says about the wrath of God: though this deserves extensive development, we can only mention it. As noted earlier, the declaration that God is love ultimately entails God's relational being; it means that God is eternally in relationship. Again, as Richard of St. Victor argued, the assertion that God is love ultimately rests on the fact that God is Trinity.[56] Failure to come to grips with the Trinity as persons in eternal self-giving relationships of love is perhaps the greatest failure of the Western church. In trying to find the essence of God *behind* the Trinity, God was depersonalized. A non-relational concept of holiness took the place of personhood, love, and relationship in our thinking about God. Beside holiness was placed justice, and with these two concepts in tandem the personal covenantal God of Israel was exchanged for a Roman judge who exacts vengeance for every misdeed of man. Ironically, in this framework the great revelation of God as the beneficent, loving, merciful Father who desires intimate relationship with his children cannot stand; it is, in practice, lost.

During the past couple of decades tremendous advances have been made in brain research. In particular, medical researchers have discovered that the human brain is hard-wired for two primal emotions: fear and love. I find it significant that one of the most oft-repeated phrases in the Scriptures is "Fear not." It seems equally significant that when the *koinonia*, or fellowship, that Adam and Eve shared with God was broken, love was replaced with fear. God is the one who seeks out humanity; his mercy and compassion are visceral (witness the father of the prodigal son). Psychologists have discovered that true change occurs in an atmosphere of unconditional love and acceptance as opposed to fear and condemnation. God does not relate to us out of conditional or contractual love. There is no condemnation for those who are in Christ Jesus! (Rom. 8:1).

---

56. Richard of St. Victor, *Richard of St Victor*, trans. Grover Zinn (New York: Paulist 1979), 374–79.

If God's action in the incarnation shows us how to understand his love, it also shows us how to understand his wrath. God is indeed angered and fiercely indignant at the way our sin has enslaved us, his children, and distorted our view of him. But his wrath against the sin that destroys us has expressed itself in going to the utmost length to break its hold on us—by giving himself to us in the incarnation. The incarnation becomes the concrete demonstration, par excellence, of divine love, compassion, humility, and self-giving. God is not a judge seeking to punish, but a compassionate Father who has picked up the tab for his wayward children and watches eagerly for them to come home. As numerous theologians (even some in the Reformed tradition!) have observed over the centuries, God loves us more than he loves himself!

Jesus' Vicarious Humanity

Christian Kettler has asked, "As common as it has been to consider Christ's death to be vicarious, carried out in our place and for us, what if we were to consider that the entirety of his humanity was lived vicariously for us and in our place?"[57] James Cassidy has summarized this concept as follows: "Jesus Christ lives for man vicariously, such that all he is and does, he is and does for us. If we want to know where our justification is, we find it in Christ. If we want to know where our faith is, we look to Christ who believed for us. Christ is objectively our all and all."[58]

"Vicarious" is not a word found in our everyday vocabulary. We have perhaps heard of parents living vicariously through their children, feeling or taking pleasure in their children's accomplishments as if they were their own. If we go to a horror movie or thriller, we feel the thrill of the action vicariously although it is happening to the character in the

---

57. Christian Kettler, *The God Who Believes* (Eugene, OR: Cascade, 2005), x. The concept of the vicarious humanity of Christ is not new. Calvin sees Christ as entering the depths of fallen humanity and redeeming it from within through his vicarious humanity. This theme was taken up in the nineteenth and twentieth centuries by John McLeod Campbell, Thomas F. Torrance, James B. Torrance, and numerous others, but its roots are found in the writings of the church fathers (especially Athanasius), echoed in Calvin's concept of the "wonderful exchange" and in Jonathan Edwards's description of the "admirable conjunction of diverse excellencies."

58. James J. Cassidy, "T. F. Torrance's Realistic Soteriological Objectivism and the Elimination of Dualisms: Union with Christ in Current Perspective," *Mid-America Journal of Theology* 19 (2008): 166.

movie and not to us. And if we have grown up in church (as I did), we have heard of the vicarious death of Christ, how his death on the cross paid the penalty for our sin so we could be forgiven and not have to suffer eternal damnation. But while the concept of the vicarious death of Christ is true and vital, standing alone it reduces the significance of Christ's death because it focuses on his work rather than his person. The work is what it is only because of the person who did the work.

It is only in the past few decades that we have seen contemporary theologians look at the "who" rather than just the "how" question. Kettler goes on to say: "The nature of Christ's vicarious work is not simply one moment on the cross, but his entire life, so that the entirety of our lives might be affected. The Word took on the entirety of humanity, body and soul, in order to save the entire human."[59]

In theology everything depends on understanding *who Jesus Christ is*, rather than just looking at *what he has done*. Unless we ask the right question, we will never get to the heart of the gospel. Even when we do ask the right question, "Who is Jesus?" we must ask it on his terms, not on our terms and based on our expectations. Jesus cannot be known outside himself, and the truth of his being is not ratified by any other means than himself. He is self-attesting. He is God, and it is only through God and on divine terms that God can be known.[60] We cannot

---

59. Kettler, *The God Who Believes*, 6. I repeat here the quote from Calvin cited earlier in a different context:

Now someone asks, How has Christ abolished sin, banished the separation between us and God, and acquired righteousness to render God favorable and kindly toward us? To this we can in general reply that *he has achieved this for us by the whole course of his obedience*. This is proved by Paul's testimony: "As by one man's disobedience many were made sinners, so by one man's obedience we are made righteous" [Rom. 5:19]. In another passage, to be sure, *Paul extends the basis of the pardon that frees us from the curse of the law to the whole life of Christ*: "But when the fullness of time came, God sent forth his Son, born of woman, subject to the law, to redeem those who were under the law" [Gal. 4:4–5]. Thus in his very baptism, also, he asserted that he fulfilled a part of righteousness in obediently carrying out his Father's commandment [Matt. 3:15]. *In short, from the time when he took on the form of a servant, he began to pay the price of liberation in order to redeem us*. (Calvin, *Institutes*, 2.16.5. Philadelphia: Westminster, 1960. Italics added.)

60. Andrew Purves, "Who Is the Incarnate Savior of the World?" in *An Introduction to Torrance Theology: Discovering the Incarnate Savior*, ed. Garrett Scott Dawson (Edinburgh: T & T Clark, 2007), 24.

know Christ simply by looking at his works. If we were to look at what Jesus did, we would probably conclude that he was a prophet endowed with special powers—that he was "the prophet like unto Moses" (Deut. 18:15; Acts 7:37–38). We could never conclude by looking at his works alone that Jesus is God.

When the author of Ecclesiastes says there is "nothing new under the sun" (1:9), he is speaking of a general principle rather than an absolute reality. In the incarnation we see a unique event. I am using the word "unique" in its proper sense to mean "one-of-a-kind," not just "uncommon." As with every statement, when we say that God never changes, we must qualify what we mean by those words. In the incarnation we have a new, one-of-a-kind event in history, and *a new experience for God himself.* Through the Son, the eternal *Logos*, God has joined himself once and forever to humanity.

The concept of the vicarious humanity of Christ is not commonly taught or even recognized today, but it is found in the historical church's teachings beginning in the second century. We see this understanding of Christ's person in the writings of Irenaeus, the missionary bishop and opponent of Gnosticism. It is developed more fully in Athanasius. Calvin expands Athanasius's understanding, calling the vicarious humanity of Christ the "wonderful exchange":

> This is the wonderful exchange which, out of his measureless benevolence, he has made with us; that, becoming Son of Man with us, he has made us sons of God with him; that, by his descent to earth, he has prepared an ascent to heaven for us; that, by taking on our mortality, he has conferred his immortality upon us; that, accepting our weakness, he has strengthened us by his power; that, receiving our poverty upon himself, he has transferred his wealth to us; that, taking the weight of our iniquity upon himself (which oppressed us), he has clothed us with his righteousness.[61]

The concept is picked up again in the nineteenth century by Scottish theologian John McLeod Campbell, and in the twentieth century by Thomas Torrance, James Torrance, and numerous others.

---

61. Calvin, *Institutes*, 4.17.2.

What does the *vicarious humanity* of Christ mean? What is its significance? Certainly we need to define it. What is commonly communicated within evangelicalism is that Jesus is the perfect sacrifice for our sins. He was holy, sinless, and perfect, reflecting the Old Testament requirement for a spotless sacrifice for sin. This is indeed a biblical theme, developed particularly in the book of Hebrews. But what has been forgotten is that Jesus was not just the vicarious sacrifice. He was *the vicarious man*, and as such represented all mankind in the same way that Adam did. Not just his death but the entirety of his human existence was on our behalf and has salvific effect for us. In other words, *there is an indissoluble unity between who Jesus is and what he does.*

> The vicarious humanity of Christ does not mean that Christ's humanity is unreal. Quite the contrary! It does mean that the vicarious humanity of Christ speaks of the deep interaction between Christ's humanity and our humanity at the level of our *being*, the *ontological* level. So the atoning work of Christ is neither simply a means by which we are declared righteous by God, nor simply a demonstration of God's love. It is both, but much more, in the sense of God desiring to re-create our humanity at the deepest levels, addressing our needs and fears, our doubts from within our very being.[62]

In evangelicalism Jesus is often treated as an "instrument" in the atonement; when the work of the instrument is done, it is placed back in the toolbox, so to speak. So when we speak of Jesus our mediator and Savior, we think mostly of his death and resurrection, and if we think of his ascension we think of it only in terms of his intercession for us in heaven so as to plead with God on our behalf by virtue of his sacrifice on the cross. We think little about his having lived life on earth for us, and even less of his ongoing life for us as an ascended and glorified human being. Atonement as we understand it has to do with the legal problem of guilt and its expiation by the shedding of blood. While that is a true understanding, to see this as the sole reason for the incarnation is hopelessly reductionistic. It ignores the depth of

---

62. Kettler, *The God Who Believes*, 6.

suffering that Jesus endured while learning obedience here on earth, as referenced in Hebrews (4:15–5:8), as well as his continuing significance and role as the God-man, the mediator between God and man—worshiping for us and bringing us with him into the joy and communion of God's presence. Jesus did not lay aside his humanity at the ascension; in his eternal existence he continues to represent us as a man.

The eternal Word, the second person of the Trinity, did indeed assume a flesh like ours in every way in order to redeem us by purifying it—by being, in our flesh, the kind of faithful human being we failed to be. In taking our flesh he was *completely* like us. But he was "completely *unlike us* in that by taking our fallen human nature upon himself, he condemned sin in it; overcame its temptations, resisted its downward drag in alienation from God, and converted it back to himself to obedience toward God, thus sanctifying it."[63] In doing this he transformed human nature and brought it again into true *koinonia* with God.

> "Standing in our place" (Latin, *vicarius*, "substitute"). Christ in his humanity stands in our place and represents us, and hence the term the "*vicarious humanity*" of Christ in which the humanity of Christ takes our place and represents us, so that what is true of him is true of us, and what he did in (our) humanity is ours.[64]

In other words, in his incarnation—encompassing his birth, ministry, death, resurrection, and ascension—the incarnate Word of God has decisively transformed humanity and become literally the head of a new humanity, centered in the one Paul calls the "last Adam" who has objectively gathered humanity into himself. This is what Paul means when he says that "in Christ God was reconciling the world to himself" (2 Cor. 5:19–20). In the late second century Irenaeus testified of the vicarious humanity of Christ:

---

63. Thomas F. Torrance, *Incarnation: The Person and Life of Christ*, ed. Robert T. Walker (Downers Grove, IL: InterVarsity Press, 2008), 205.
    64. Ibid.

For it was for this end that the Word of God was made man, and He who was the Son of God became the Son of Man, that man, having been taken into the Word, and receiving the adoption, might become the Son of God. For by no other means could we have attained to incorruptibility and immortality, unless we had been united to incorruptibility and immortality. But how could we be joined to incorruptibility and immortality, unless, first, incorruptibility and immortality had become that which we also are, so that the corruptible might be swallowed up by incorruptibility and the mortal by immortality, that we might receive the adoption of sons?[65]

The vicarious humanity of Christ is ultimately grounded in the concept of the Word being *homoousios* with the Father. As noted earlier, this concept is often referred to simply as the *homoousion*. It is because of the *homoousion* that Jesus can say, "I and the Father are one" (John 10:30) and "If you have seen me you have seen the Father" (14:9). The other side of the equation is what is referred to in theology as the *hypostatic union*. This is the true unity not just of deity in the abstract as a sort of divine essence, but of *the second person of the Trinity* with true humanity in one person, Jesus of Nazareth. He is *homoousios* with us as to his human nature.[66]

The unity of Jesus as God and man is expressed in the Chalcedonian Creed (451): Jesus is

consubstantial with the Father as to his godhead, and consubstantial also with us as to his manhood; like unto us in all things, yet without sin . . . to be acknowledged in two natures, inconfusedly, unchangeably, indivisibly, inseparably; the distinction of natures being by no means taken away by the union, but rather the property of each nature being preserved, and concurring in

---

65. Irenaeus, "Against Heresies," III, 19.i, in *Ante-Nicene Fathers*, vol. 1, ed. Philip Schaff (Garland, TX: Galaxie Software, 2000).

66. The term *homoousios* is used twice in the Chalcedonian Creed—once to affirm unity with God the Father as to Christ's deity, and once to speak of his unity with humanity.

one Person and one Subsistence, not parted or divided into two persons, but one and the same Son.[67]

It is because of this dual nature that Jesus stands on both sides of the covenant: God's and ours. In this capacity he acts simultaneously not only as our substitute—*instead of* us—but also our representative—*as* us. The scope of this representative ministry is stunning. In our fallen condition we can do nothing of ourselves; as Jesus said in the upper room discourse, "apart from me you can do nothing" (John 15:5). His entire life is offered up to the Father as a perfect response to the covenant. He is *the representative human*, so that our humanity is now intertwined with his. All of Jesus' human activity is ours vicariously because we are in union with him (*en Christo*). As Watchman Nee has observed,

> When therefore the Lord Jesus was crucified on the cross, he was crucified as the last Adam. All that was in the first Adam was gathered up and done away in him. We were included there. As the last Adam he wiped out the old race; as the second Man he brings in the new race.[68]

Let us take faith as an example. Most of us understand faith as something we do or perform autonomously, independently, with its origin within ourselves. Even if we understand it as a gift of God, it is ours and we must exercise it as our response to what Christ has done. But because of his vicarious humanity, Jesus receives the summons to have faith in God, to believe and trust in God, and responds to it; he exercises faith in our place and as our representative from within the depths of our unfaithfulness, providing us with a faithfulness in which we may share.

> [Our] response of faith [to God] should not begin with the weakness and vacillation of our faith, but with the faith of Jesus, a faith that is part of his wider human response in every way, even including our repentance. [Jesus'] solidarity [with us]

---

67. Philip Schaff, *History of the Christian Church*, vol. 3 (Garland, TX: Galaxie Software, 2002).

68. Watchman Nee, *The Normal Christian Life* (Wheaton, IL: Tyndale, 1977), 47.

is the means for Christ to be our substitute. . . . Jesus the Son of God must walk the path of sinful humanity, sharing in our stories, including our doubts and fears. This is the path of both representing our humanity and taking our place.[69]

He fulfills both sides of the covenant: both God's faithfulness to man and the human response of faithfulness to God. Our faith and our faithfulness partake of Christ's.

The biblical evidence for this is found in numerous New Testament passages, the most prominent of which is Galatians 2:20, properly translated: "the life I now live . . . I live because of the faithfulness of the Son of God."[70]

This does not depersonalize the human faith response but enhances the "humanness" of it. Torrance states, "because the incarnate Son of God is fully human [*enhypostasis*],[71] his response personalizes ours" so it can "issue freely and spontaneously out of our own human life before God." So the work of Christ in his vicarious humanity never diminishes the human person but upholds the dignity of the response of faith. "In faith it is upon the faithfulness of Christ that we rest and even the way in which we rest on him is sustained and undergirded by his unfailing faithfulness."[72]

Such an understanding of human faith precludes the temptation to

---

69. Kettler, *The God Who Believes*, 27.

70. Most recent translations have rendered Galatians 2:20 as faith in the Son of God. However, Calvin, in his commentaries, also translated these passages as "faithfulness of" rather than "faith in." During the past century New Testament exegetes have increasingly agreed with Calvin here.

71. "The human nature of Jesus Christ is in fact a nature joined to a person, and therefore enhypostatic, or personalized. But the person who personalizes the human nature of Christ is not a created human person (like all the other persons personalizing the other human natures we encounter); rather it is the eternal second person of the Trinity. So the human nature of Christ is personal, but with a personhood from above." Fred Sanders and Klaus Issler, eds., *Jesus in Trinitarian Perspective* (Nashville: B & H Academic, 2007), 31.

72. Myk Habets, "Evangelical Calvinism, pt. 2: Vicarious Humanity" (http://theologicalrefelection.wordpress.com/tag/myk-habets/).

have faith in our faith—that is, faith in faith itself, rather than faith in Christ. "Our faith is altogether grounded in him who is 'author and finisher,' on whom faith depends from start to finish."[73]

---

73 Ibid.

Chapter 6

The Holy Spirit

> We believe in the Holy Spirit, the Lord, the giver of life,
> who proceeds from the Father [and the Son],
> who with the Father and the Son is worshiped and glorified,
> who has spoken through the prophets.
>
> —*Nicene-Constantinopolitan Creed*

Throughout the nearly two millennia that the church has been in existence, there have been countless studies on God and on the person and work of Christ. In the apostolic church we find that the Holy Spirit was vital and active, but after the close of the apostolic era the Holy Spirit seems to fade into the background. In many respects the Holy Spirit became the forgotten member of the godhead.

By the late second century, the dynamic and freedom of the Spirit had in large measure yielded to the growing institutionalization of the church under the authority of the bishops. This downplaying of the supernatural activity of the Spirit brought forth a protest movement in the form of Montanism,[1] which sought to re-infuse the church with the early dynamic of the Spirit. Montanism was schismatic rather than overtly heretical, but the established church nevertheless soundly

---

1. Montanism was a late second-century ecstatic/prophetic, apocalyptic, and ascetic movement founded by a priest called Montanus, a recently converted pagan from Phrygia (northern Asia Minor). While the sect affirmed orthodox theological tenets, its extreme emphasis on prophecy coupled with asceticism and the courting of martyrdom brought opposition and eventual condemnation by synods in Rome and Asia.

149

rejected it. Despite the diminishment of the Spirit's work beginning in the second century, however, the literature of the first several centuries tells us that it did not cease with the death of the apostles. We find account after account of the miraculous work of the Spirit, particularly in evangelistic efforts aimed at the pagan tribes outside the empire. The history of the church throughout the ancient and early medieval periods is filled with accounts of miracles of all types testifying to the ongoing work of the Spirit.[2]

We find among the early church fathers a tacit admission that the Holy Spirit was not central in the church's theological understanding, which focused instead on the relationship between the Father and the Son. In fact, in the Nicene Creed (325) we find opening statements about God the Father, then a larger focus on the person of Christ and his eternal relationship to the Father, and only a single assertion at the end concerning the Spirit: "and we believe in the Holy Spirit." The version of the Nicene Creed repeated today actually comes from the Council of Constantinople in 381; in it the statement on the Holy Spirit is expanded, making explicit the Spirit's position and function as the third member of the Trinity: "And in the Holy Spirit, the Lord and Giver of life, who proceeds from the Father, who with the Father and the Son together is worshiped and glorified, who spoke by the prophets."

---

2. In the early church in Acts we see miracles on a regular basis. While miracles (according to records) seem to be much less frequent by the late second century, there continue to be historical reports of miracles throughout the medieval period. The third-century bishop Gregory of Neocaesarea in Asia Minor is reputed to have performed so many miracles that he was given the title Thaumaturgus (literally, "Wonderworker"). Gregory's life is one of the best authenticated in ancient times, and numerous non-Christian historians admit that his miracles ought not to be doubted. Likewise Martin of Tours performed many miracles in his ministry in rural Gaul, particularly miracles that demonstrated Christ's power over pagan deities. Oxford-educated historian Richard Fletcher says of the accounts of medieval miracles, "Like it or not, this is what our sources tell us over and over again. Demonstrations of the power of the Christian God meant conversion. Miracles, wonders, exorcisms, temple-torching and shrine-smashing *were in and of themselves* acts of evangelism" (Richard Fletcher, *The Barbarian Conversions* [New York: Henry Holt, 1997], 45). In fact, we regularly find reports of the miraculous, particularly in areas where the gospel confronts paganism. We children of the Enlightenment are naturally skeptical because we inhabit a worldview that is essentially deistic and mechanistic. Our worldview is not that of the ancient world and particularly not that of the Scriptures.

The person and work of the Holy Spirit was so much overshadowed by the focus on the Father and the Son that the church fathers referred to the Holy Spirit as the "modesty of God." The same phenomenon continues today; I have recently obtained a book for my library entitled *The Holy Spirit: Shy Member of the Trinity.*[3] The Holy Spirit was in those early centuries understood to be working behind the scenes, facilitating relationships while deflecting attention away from himself and toward Christ. Yet the picture of the Spirit that we get through a careful reading of Scripture as well as a closer look into history is one of unpredictable activity, creativity, and change.

The Holy Spirit in the Old Testament

The Spirit of God first appears in the early verses of Genesis 1: "Now the earth was without shape and empty, and darkness was over the surface of the watery deep, but the Spirit of God was moving over the surface of the water" (v. 2).[4] It is interesting that the New English Bible (1970) speaks not of the "Spirit of God" but rather of "a mighty wind that swept over the surface of the waters."[5] This is because the

---

3. Frederick Dale Bruner and William Hordern, *The Holy Spirit: Shy Member of the Trinity* (Eugene OR: Wipf & Stock, 2001).

4. *The NET Bible: First Edition* (Richardson, TX: Biblical Studies Press, 2006).

5. Here the New English Bible presents an interpretation of Genesis 1:1–2 favored by many Old Testament scholars since about 1920. The grammar is interpreted in line with the opening verses of other ancient Near Eastern stories of creation, such as the Babylonian *Enuma Elish*, which begins, "When above, the heavens had not been named, and below, the earth had not been called by name . . ." Also, the *ruach* of God is understood as a "wind" rather than his "Spirit." On the alleged parallels with the Babylonian myth, see the full discussion by Alexander Heidel in his book *The Babylonian Genesis* (Chicago: University of Chicago Press, 1951). But many other scholars have not been convinced that the opening verses of Genesis should be understood in this way. The translators of the Revised Standard Version's Old Testament (1953) declined to adopt the new interpretation, although they indicate it in their footnotes. It should be noted that, in addition to other elements of the Babylonian interpretation, the New English Bible has here interpreted the "wind *of God*" as "a mighty wind," but this interpretation of the word *elohim* is questionable. Harry Olinski in his *Notes on the New Translation of the Torah* (Philadelphia: The Jewish Publication Society, 1969) observes that "there is no authority for this in any tradition" and "the word *elohim* does not have the meaning 'mighty, tempestuous,' or the like in a single one of the some 2,570 occurrences of the word in the Bible" (55) (http://www.bible-researcher.com/neb.html).

translators were drawing on parallels with *Enuma Elish* (also known as *The Babylonian Genesis*, a text discovered by archeologists in the late nineteenth century) and operating under the then popular view that the Genesis account relied on Babylonian creation myths. The Hebrew term *ruach* can indeed be translated "wind" and "breath" as well as "spirit" and "Spirit"; we find the same phenomenon in the New Testament, where the Greek term *pneuma* is variously translated "wind," "breeze," "breath," "spirit," or "Spirit," depending on the context. But both the immediate and the larger contexts of Scripture lead us to conclude that it is not "a mighty wind" that is in view in Genesis 1:2. In the immediate context, the verb translated "moving" (NET, NASB) or "hovering" (ESV) is typically used of a bird hovering or brooding over her young (see also Deut. 32:11). It is interesting that in John 3 we see Jesus playing on the dual meaning of the term *pneuma*, using it to refer alternately to wind and Spirit so as to emphasize the freedom, unpredictability, and invisibility of the Sprit's activity.

As Christians we read the term "Spirit of God" and immediately understand it to refer to the Holy Spirit, the third person of the Trinity. Clearly the Israelites did not understand God to be tri-personal; as we have noted earlier, the *Shema* in Deuteronomy 6:4 says, "Hear, O Israel, YHWH our *Elohim*, YHWH is one." Throughout the Hebrew Scriptures the Spirit is understood by the Jews as an impersonal force that goes out from YHWH, as opposed to the person of the Holy Spirit who is referenced and described in the New Testament. In the Old Testament, images of God and his activity reflect a pre-Trinitarian understanding since they were written before the incarnation. In these texts we see God's powerful activity represented in images such as fire, light, water, and wind (*ruach*). "Spirit" is a general term used to speak of divine activity and presence.[6] As Clark Pinnock has observed:

---

6. When we speak of a religion, culture, tradition, or people, we must not understand that group monolithically. This is demonstrably true of first-century Judaism and also of the Second Temple Judaism of the intertestamental period. On the one hand, for example, a significant part of the Jewish people succumbed to the underlying Greek worldview that reduced piety to a legalistic performance of the minutiae of the Law while missing that to which the Law pointed, but there were also other traditions represented by the Qumran community. In the Second Temple period there was some discussion among the rabbis about the possibility of plurality in the Godhead; however, after the rise of Christianity with its insistence on the Trinity,

Non-Trinitarians are right to say that God is spirit and that when we encounter spirit we encounter God himself. Spirit can refer to divine immanence, as opposed to a reference to a distinct Person in the godhead. Liberalism was right to associate spirit with the general presence of God in the world, because it often refers to precisely that and to our experience of communion with God. As spirit, God inspires, motivates and empowers people everywhere.

It would be a mistake, however, to deny other texts that use Spirit in a distinctly Trinitarian way. For in addition to evidence that God is spirit, there is ample evidence to support the claim that God has Spirit in a Trinitarian sense. It is a little confusing for one term to refer to two related realities, i.e., for God's incorporeal being and his general immanent presence in creation as well as the personal presence of the third person of the triune God, but it is so. Perhaps there is a reason for this rooted in the Spirit's chosen identity in the history of salvation. Perhaps Spirit wishes no other name than the generic ascription for God. The others are called "Father" and "Son," but Spirit takes no special name and chooses to remain anonymous.[7]

Looking at the Old Testament today with the fuller understanding of New Testament revelation, we find there the fingerprints of the immanent personal presence of the triune God in the person of the Holy Spirit, as we do also in the New Testament.

---

mainstream Judaism ceased such speculation and retreated into absolute monotheism. Following the destruction of the Temple and the end of the sacrificial system, a mystical strain of Judaism arose among certain of the rabbis; according to tradition, Rabbi Shimon Bar Yochai (of the second and third centuries) compiled the *Zohar*, the foundational text for mystical Jewish thought of the Kabbalah. The book appeared in Spain during the eleventh century and became a vital part of the Kabbalistic tradition. During the nineteenth century, Hirsch Prinz, a converted rabbi using the pseudonym Rabbi Tzviz Nassi, wrote *The Great Mystery* or *How can Three Be One?*, which traces the concept of the Trinity through the *Zohar*. See http://nazarenespace.com/profiles/blogs/the-great-mystery-or-how-can.

7. Clark Pinnock, *The Flame of Love* (Downers Grove, IL: InterVarsity Press, 1996), 25–26.

We theologians have as part of our "job description"[8] the construction of doctrine out of the biblical material, which then becomes part of our belief system. But when it comes to an understanding of the Spirit, the very nature of the topic ultimately defies codification. Theologians deal with rational concepts, with ideas as opposed to the existential. But the Spirit as described in Scripture is existential to the core.

> The concept *rûaḥ* is an existential term. At its heart is the *experience* of a mysterious, awesome power—the mighty invisible force of the wind, the mystery of vitality, the otherly power that transforms—all *rûaḥ*, all manifestations of divine energy.[9]

The Development of a Trinitarian Understanding of the Spirit

In light of the reality that the church understands the Spirit as a full person co-equal with the Father and the Son, it is amazing that the Holy Spirit has played such a small role overall in theological discussion over the centuries. Given this fact, it is supremely ironic that the separation of the Eastern (Orthodox) and Western (Catholic) churches into two competing communions (which excommunicated each other in 1054) was over a seemingly minor point of Trinitarian understanding relating to the Holy Spirit: specifically, how the Holy Spirit is related to the Father and the Son in their intra-Trinitarian being.

As noted earlier, the great contribution of the Council of Nicaea (325) was the term *homoousios*. The term occurs in the Nicene Creed with reference to the eternal relationship of the Father to the Son and the Son to the Father. Again, it means literally that the Father and the Son are of the same "being," or "essence," and was used to express the fact that the Son is equally God with the Father. He is no less divine in his *being* than the Father; he is in no sense a secondary God, or derived from the Father by the Father's will. He did not come into being by a

---

8. See chapter 2 of my *Survivor's Guide to Theology* (Grand Rapids: Zondervan, 2006) for a discussion of the theological task.

9. D. R. W. Wood and I. H. Marshall, eds., *New Bible Dictionary*, 3rd ed. (Downers Grove, IL: InterVarsity Press, 1996), 1125.

decision of the Father. As God, his relationship to the Father is eternal and necessary.

In contrast to their focus on the Father-Son relationship and its implications, the Nicene fathers referenced the Spirit in a simple line, almost a footnote in the creed: "And we believe in the Holy Spirit." It was not that the church at the time was *binitarian* as opposed to *Trinitarian*, believing formally in the deity of only the Father and the Son and not the Spirit; rather, the raging theological issue at the time revolved around the full deity of the Son, and the practical implications of this reality or its denial. It was simply that the relationship of the Spirit was not then in view. Over the following fifty-six years the relationship of the Spirit to the Father and the Son did come into view, and became a topic of debate. In its reaffirmation and further refinement of the creed, the Council of Constantinople (381) stated: "We believe in the Holy Spirit, the Lord and giver of life, who proceeds from the Father, who with the Father and Son is to be worshiped and glorified." This is hardly a full discussion of the Spirit, but the affirmation that the Spirit is to be worshiped along with the Father and the Son testifies that he, too, is *homoousios* with the Father and the Son.

The question of how the persons of the Trinity were to be related was not formally addressed in the creed. But proposals, discussions, and debates were ongoing among many of the Nicene fathers. After Nicaea had affirmed the full deity of the persons of the Trinity, one of the pressing questions became how to avoid the charge of tritheism.

Perichoresis

The major work stemmed from Athanasius, who saw the implications of *homoousios* as relating to the essential *being* of God. It has long been recognized that Athanasius, the Cappadocians,[10] and several other fourth-century Eastern fathers began their theological Trinitarian reasoning with the "threeness" of God and worked to a unity. The question was how to explain the unity. All saw the Father as the logical starting point; the Scripture denoted the Son as "begotten" by the Father. The Spirit on the other hand was understood to *proceed* from the Father.[11]

---

10. Basil the Great, Gregory of Nyssa, and Gregory of Nazianzus.

11. The Nicene fathers never explain what "proceeds" means; rather, it became a

As noted in the previous chapter, the explanation developed by Gregory of Nazianzus was what would come to be known as *perichoresis*,[12] the concept of the three persons of the Trinity "indwelling" each other and interpenetrating each other. In explaining the importance of the Trinity, Tim Keller has stated, "Each of the divine persons centers upon the others. None demands that the others revolve around him. Each voluntarily circles the other two, pouring love, delight, and adoration into them. Each person of the Trinity loves, adores, defers to,

---

way to distinguish the relationship of the Son to the Father from that of the Spirit to the Father. Gregory of Nazianzus declares essentially that the only way the three members of the Trinity are to be distinguished or identified is by "origin":

The Father is Father, and is Unoriginate, for He is of no one; the Son is Son, and is not Unoriginate, for He is of the Father. But if you take the word Origin in a temporal sense, He too is Unoriginate, for He is the Maker of Time, and is not subject to Time. The Holy Ghost is truly Spirit, coming forth from the Father indeed, but not after the manner of the Son, for it is not by Generation but by Procession (since I must coin a word for the sake of clearness); for neither did the Father cease to be Unbegotten because of His begetting something, nor the Son to be begotten because He is of the Unbegotten (how could that be?), nor is the Spirit changed into Father or Son because He proceeds, or because He is God. ("Oration 39.12," in *Nicene and Post-Nicene Fathers*, series 2, vol.7 (Grand Rapids: Eerdmans, 1974), 356.

12. *Perichoresis* was first used as a theological term by Gregory of Nazianzus (329–389) , who employed it with reference to the human and divine natures of Christ co-existing in one person without becoming merged into a single divine-human nature lacking the distinctive properties of each. About two centuries later, a student of Gregory's writings named Maximus the Confessor picked up and refined the concept of *perichoresis*. The next reference that we can find is in a treatise on the Trinity whose author is known to scholars as Pseudo-Cyril of Alexandra. John of Damascus (d. 749), who wrote an important treatise called *The Orthodox Faith*, picked up the term from Pseudo-Cyril's work and through him it became a technical theological term used in both East and West. Importantly, however, Thomas F. Torrance notes that "once *perichoresis* is refined and changed to apply to the Trinity . . . it can no longer be applied to Christology at the lower level, to express the union between the divine and the human natures in Christ, without serious damage to the doctrine of Christ" (Thomas F. Torrance, *The Ground and Grammar of Theology* [New York: T & T Clark 1980], 173). G. L. Prestige, an early church scholar, contends that there are two distinct meanings to the term *perichoresis*, the first being "interchange" or "reciprocity" and the other being "interpenetration." He sees the second as a later and more technical meaning. Prestige notes that the use of the term to mean "interpenetration" "is an admirable description of the Persons of God. And it was necessary to find some such simple and expressive term for the purpose . . . Without such a definition, the recurrence of tritheism was almost inevitable" (G. L. Prestige, *God in Patristic Thought* [London: SPCK, 1959], 297). To this it should be added that the term also ruled out modalism.

and rejoices in the others. That creates a dynamic, pulsating dance of joy and love."[13] One blogger pictures the relationship as a kind of dance in a different context:

> Perichoresis describes the three persons, God the Father, the Son and Holy Spirit, three distinct persons, but all of one "ousia" or essence, indwelling in each other, partaking in each other, and "dancing" around each other in a creative, spontaneous dance of love and joy and relationship . . . The explanation of it reminds me of the "dance" that takes place in some aikido dojos when three people are practicing and entering and exiting the other's space—it's a beautiful thing to watch.[14]

Procession of the Spirit

The Nicene fathers envisioned the person of God under the concept of *Archē*, the Greek term denoting origin or source. This is a metaphor that runs through all of Scripture from Genesis to Revelation. God is the origin and source of all creation, beginning with the creation account of Genesis 1; given that the Greco-Roman world saw matter as eternal and the creator as a mere demiurge, an architect and craftsman as opposed to one who created *ex nihilo* (out of nothing), Hebrews 11:3 eliminates any residual ambiguity in the Genesis 1 account by stipulating that God did not create the world out of material that was already there. This concept of *Archē* played a key role in the development of the understanding of the relationship and distinctions between the persons of the Trinity. At

---

13. Tim Keller, *The Reason for God* (New York: Dutton, 2008), loc. 212, Kindle ed.

14. Mike Ferruggia, "Perichoresis and the Holy Trinity" (https://taichimike. wordpress.com/2010/02/08/perichoresis-and-the-holy-trinity/) .

To explain this a bit further: *perichoresis (perichoresis, circumincessio)* is a theological term that describes the "necessary being-in-one-another or circumincession of the three divine Persons of the Trinity because of the single divine essence, the eternal [begetting] of the Son from the Father and the Spirit [proceeding] from the Father and (through) the Son, and the fact that the three Persons are distinguished solely by the relations of opposition between them." This term was popularized in the eighth century by John of Damascus who, in his *De fide orthodoxa*, said that the three persons of the Trinity "are made one not so as to commingle, but so as to cleave to each other, and they have their being in each other [*kai ten en allelais perichoresin*] without any coalescence or commingling."

the risk of becoming somewhat technical, the following paragraphs will explore this in order to provide a context for the differences between the Eastern (Greek) and the Western (Latin—encompassing both Catholic and Protestant) understandings of the Trinity.

The term "Father" is used in the New Testament with reference to God the Father. Likewise "God" usually has reference to the Father, but sometimes may refer to the whole Trinity. Athanasius, drawing on the concept of *homoousia*, concluded that since the "whole godhead is in the Son and in the Spirit [as well as in the Father], they must be included with the Father as the originless Source or *Archē* of the Holy Trinity."[15] The three Cappadocian theologians, however, took a different path to expound their Trinitarian understanding. Unlike Athanasius and several of his contemporaries, they did not begin with the concept of *homoousia*; rather, they began their explanation with the concept of God as tri-personal (i.e., three individual persons, or *hypostases*) to expound the specific modes of existence of each person of the Trinity. The net effect was to do justice to each person more fully, but "at the expense of cutting out the real meaning of *ousia* as '*being*' in internal relations."[16] To spell this out more clearly: in their desire to define more precisely the persons of the Trinity, the Cappadocians focused on the individuality of the persons of the godhead. In so doing their explanations stretched the individuality of the Trinitarian persons and minimized the equality they share because of their common *being*, that is, the *homoousion*. The Cappadocian understanding was implicitly rejected by the Council of Constantinople, which reaffirmed the terminology of the Nicene Creed, adopting it to speak of the *relationship among* the Trinitarian persons without explicitly referring to "persons" (*hypostases*).

Yet as Eastern Trinitarian theology developed, the Cappadocian understanding was progressively embraced by later Eastern fathers.[17] The

---

15. Thomas F. Torrance, *The Christian Doctrine of God: One Being, Three Persons* (Edinburgh: T & T Clark, 1996), 181. This position was also expounded by Hilary and Epiphanius.

16. Ibid.

17. Thomas F. Torrance notes the danger of rigid definitions in his audio lectures on "The Ground and Grammar of Theology" delivered at Fuller Seminary in 1981. Using the example of Athanasius as opposed to the Cappadocians, he says that "once

Cappadocian understanding, along with the Athanasian one, rightly rejected the subordination of the Son and the Spirit in their *being* to the Father (i.e., the notion that the Son and the Spirit were somehow less God than the Father), who was the source of all. It was this idea of subordination, a fundamental component of Arianism, that had plagued the pre-Nicene fathers in speaking of the relations between the Father and the Son; the terminology of the creed, by asserting the *homoousion*, had eliminated subordination generally and Arianism in particular. At the same time, however, the Cappadocians did introduce a subtle hierarchy into the godhead, a hierarchy whereby the Son is begotten out of the *person* of the Father, and the Spirit proceeds out of the *person* of the Father as opposed to having their source in the *nature (ousia)* of the Father.[18] This subtle shift introduced the theological issue that eventually led to the split of Eastern and Western churches.

In the Eastern understanding the *person* (as opposed to the *being*) of the Father is the sole *archē* (source) and integration point of the Trinity and of all reality. In 589 at the Synod of Toledo (Spain), the Western church added a single word to the creed: *filioque* (Latin for "and the Son"). Instead of reading "the Holy Spirit, who proceeds from the Father," in the West the creed read, "the Holy Spirit, who proceeds from the Father *and the Son*." The West was still fighting pockets of Arianism and by adding the *filioque* to the creed sought to strengthen the affirmation of the equality of the Son and the Father. The Eastern church objected strenuously on two counts. One was political: the

---

you start defining a term you give the term some right in itself . . . Athanasius always uses terms in a flexible and dynamic way." The idea here is that all definitions must be seen as approximations, since no linguistic definition can exhaust the reality to which it refers. Athanasius sees that definitions must be loosely bounded, allowing more insight rather than being restrictive. It was exactly this restrictive use of precise definitions by the Cappadocians regarding the Trinitarian persons and essence that led to the problem of the *filioque*.

18. This grounding of the being of the persons of the Son and the Spirit in the person of the Father can be seen in the work of the leading contemporary Orthodox scholar and Metropolitan John Zizioulas. In his *Being as Communion* (New York: St. Vladimir's Seminary Press, 1985), Zizioulas argues that "the monarchy of the Father is the presupposition of the distinction between persons" (45). Miroslav Volf observes that this insistence seems to arise from Zizioulas "projecting the hierarchical grounding of unity into the doctrine of the Trinity from the perspective of a particular ecclesiology"(Miroslav Volf, *After Our Likeness* [Grand Rapids: Eerdmans, 1998], 79).

Nicene-Constantinopolitan Creed was an ecumenical, universal creed, so a local Western church synod had no right or authority to alter it unilaterally. The Council of Constantinople (381) had declared only that the Holy Spirit proceeds from the Father (see John 15:26), and any change to this wording would require a universal council.

The second objection was theological: from the Eastern perspective, the *filioque* is by implication heretical because it turns the East's understanding of the Trinity on its head. The concept of the double procession of the Spirit from both Father and Son introduced *two* ultimate sources of being into the godhead and destroyed the unity of the Trinity. Eastern theology, following the lead of the Cappadocian fathers, understands there to be a *mon*archy within the Trinity. God the Father *in his person* is the source of all. The *filioque* would be an affirmation that there were two ultimate sources of origin for one of the divine persons, the Holy Spirit, destroying the already centuries-old understanding of the unity of all things centered in the person of the Father. The Eastern church consequently labeled the *filioque* the "mother of all heresies," with the ultimate result that in 1054, the church split into the Eastern Orthodox and Catholic communions.

Consequences of the Filioque Dispute

The *filioque* has had the further unfortunate effect of subordinating the Holy Spirit to the Son, so that in effect the Spirit becomes the ignored member of the godhead. His role in the life of the church has been diminished. In the centuries following the split, the Western church took on an institutional character that domesticated the Spirit and reduced him to a power to be manipulated and dispensed by the clergy rather than a concrete expression of the divine life who in his diverse manifestations freely indwells the church as Christ's body. This in turn led to an underappreciation of diversity and an overemphasis on unity that has ultimately resulted in the centralization of ecclesiastical power in the papacy.[19]

---

19. Back in the fourth and fifth centuries in the West, Augustine was also involved in Trinitarian explication. He began with the unity or oneness of God and moved to diversity and threeness. His explanation focused on the love between the persons

Which side was right in the split? In fact, both articulations have inherent problems—problems beyond the immediate political and theological maneuvering that separated the church. The central problem strikes at the heart of the possibility of knowing God as he is in himself. Neither side has attempted to address this issue from a theological perspective. Thomas Torrance contends that the issue is not one without resolution; rather, the problem arises from the Cappadocians' ultimate grounding of the unity of the Trinity in the monarchy of the *person* of the Father rather than the *being* of the Father.

As noted, in the West the Holy Spirit was domesticated by the church so that the relational reality of the persons of the Trinity was lost. As a result the West lost contact with any kind of knowledge of God as he is in himself. The Augustinian synthesis grounded the concept of God in Neoplatonic philosophy, seeing God as utterly transcendent and personally unknowable to humanity as he is in himself.[20] Gunton shows how Augustine, failing to grasp the significance of the work of the Cappadocian theologians, through his massive influence injected into Western Trinitarian understanding a recurring tendency toward modalism, which closes off the possibility of knowing anything of God as he is in his intra-Trinitarian being.[21]

What happened in the East is a bit more complicated to trace; however, as in the West, the developments in the East overemphasized the transcendence of God the Father so that rational knowledge of him became an impossibility. As I have written elsewhere:

---

of the Father and the Son, and identified the Holy Spirit as *the bond of love* between the Father and Son. This emphasized the central role of the Spirit as the one who promotes communion or fellowship (*koinonia*). But this line of thought in Augustine is a two-edged sword: it emphasizes an essential truth about the Spirit while implicitly compromising the Spirit's full personhood in a way that is perilous to full-orbed Trinitarian understanding. Admittedly, Augustine's insight is helpful on one level— the Scriptures do present the Holy Spirit as the facilitator of relationship. It is in and through the Spirit that the Father loves the Son, and in and through the Spirit that the Son loves the Father. However, this explanation had the negative side effect of depersonalizing the Spirit by reducing him to an impersonal force. We can see the result of such depersonalization time and time again throughout the history of the church.

20. Colin Gunton, *The Promise of Trinitarian Theology*, 2nd ed. (New York: T & T Clark, 1997), 42.

21. Ibid., 30–55. Gunton's discussion is thorough.

One of the central tenets of Orthodox theology is that God in himself is absolutely transcendent and rationally unknowable. Thus he can be described only in the *apophatic* language of negation—that is, we can describe what he is *not* like rather than make positive assertions about what he *is* like; for example, "God is not finite" rather than "God is infinite." However, God can be known experientially and mystically, not in his *essence* but in his divine *energies* (his dynamic working). The emphasis in Orthodoxy is on the limitations inherent in the finiteness of the human mind, which makes it impossible for us to grasp the infinite greatness of the holy Creator. "We can say that the negative way of the knowledge of God is an intellectual experience of the mind's failure when confronted with something beyond the conceivable." This position asserts that the mystical and personal path to the knowledge of God is superior to the intellectual. While nearly all branches of Christian theology contain apophatic elements, in Orthodoxy it has become a predominant theme. . . .

In asserting that God is absolutely transcendent, the Orthodox do not deny his immanence. Rather, they assert that God exists within his creation by virtue of his divine energies. By this is meant that God himself *works* intimately and immanently in the created order while in his essence he remains apart and separate from creation. It could be said that God works in and is known and experienced through his work in creation, but personally he is totally separate from that creation. Thus arises the paradox that God is a God who hides himself while being at the same time a God who acts and who through his actions reveals himself.

This work of God in his divine energies does not imply that God in his workings is an impersonal force; he is profoundly personal. His personal nature is God's triunity. When God is apprehended in his workings, he is apprehended face to face and experienced as a personal being.[22]

This Eastern understanding has not forsworn a personal knowledge of some type, but any inkling of God as he is in himself, that is, as he

---

22. Sawyer, *The Survivor's Guide to Theology*, 242–43.

exists in his *intra-Trinitarian personal relationships*, is cut off from human knowledge.

Thus both the Eastern and the Western understandings of the Trinity have in different ways cut off any human knowledge of God as he is in himself. Thomas Torrance traces this issue in the East to the Cappadocian grounding of the persons of the Trinity in the *person* of the Father rather than in the *being* of the Father—or, to put it another way, it arises from a failure to work out the implications of the *homoousion* as taught by the Nicene-Constantinopolitan Creed with a rigorous application of the concept of *perichoresis* to understanding the persons of the Trinity. A rigorous application of these two universally accepted theological principles would not have allowed the person of God the Father to drift off into abstraction and the Holy Spirit to become depersonalized since God as he is in himself can be *truly apprehended* in the person of the incarnate Son.[23] Torrance does not assert that we can *comprehend* God as he is in himself, but we can *apprehend* him truly on account of the incarnation. We can have a true glimpse into the intra-Trinitarian being of God through our knowledge of the Son, who declared "whoever has seen me has seen the Father" (John 14:9). Torrance further asserts that the answer to this problem is to go behind the Cappadocians and back to Athanasius and the Nicene pronouncement. To do so solves the problem of the *filioque*. In fact, dialogue between the Reformed churches and the Orthodox communion has reached agreement on this issue by following this route.[24]

The Go-Between God

Theologians have long recognized that a primary ministry of the Spirit is establishing relationships. The Spirit is the divine facilitator. In the incarnation something new happened to God—the second person of the Trinity was eternally joined to humanity. This joining is not merely an external clamping together of the divine and

---

23. See Gunton's discussion of the increasing abstraction of God that took place in Western Trinitarian theology, beginning with Augustine, in *The Promise of Trinitarian Theology*, 30–55. This ultimate unknowability allowed for arbitrariness in God the Father and opened the door to such doctrines as double predestination as seen in Augustine and picked up again in the Reformation.

24. Thomas F. Torrance, *The Christian Doctrine of God*, 185.

human natures, but a true ontological union of the divine second person of the Trinity with human nature. The ministry of the Spirit is one of solidarity—in this case, of empowering the humble and newly incarnate God the Son,[25] who has assumed human weakness, to maintain his eternal communion with the Father. At the same time, as Irenaeus pointed out more than eighteen centuries ago, it was a case of the Spirit "getting used to" union with humanity. The Spirit, in anointing Jesus without measure, "got used to" living in and participating together with a man who in the weakness of his flesh nevertheless clung to his communion with the Father. Beginning at Pentecost, the Spirit has now joined himself to human beings who, although reconciled to God (Father, Son, and Spirit) and already participating in the divine life, are still existentially weak and sinful since they have not learned to live in dependence on the Spirit and in communion with the Father.

The Holy Spirit is unseen, like the wind, but his presence is not unnoticed. Likewise, as the "shy member of the Trinity" the Holy Spirit draws attention away from himself and toward Christ. The Spirit is often spoken of in terms of fellowship: the "fellowship of the Holy Spirit" is a phrase regularly used in the writings of Paul. The Spirit also illuminates and shows the beauty of that which might otherwise remain unseen. I believe a powerful illustration of one aspect of the Spirit's work can be seen in the breathtaking view of a building or a city skyline at night, lit up in a way that highlights the beauty of the architecture. It is the light that makes the difference. The Holy Spirit lights up that upon which he "shines." And like the light source that is itself unseen, he points away from himself to that which he illumines.

Salvation: Participation in the Life of God by the Spirit

The language of *participation* is virtually unknown to present-day Protestants in speaking of salvation, yet for the fathers this was a primary category in their understanding. We also see this theme in many

---

25. The ministry of the Holy Spirit in the life of Jesus is developed at length by Myk Habets in *The Anointed Son: A Trinitarian Spirit Christology* (Eugene, OR: Wipf & Stock, 2010). Clark Pinnock provides a survey of "Spirit Christology" in his *The Flame of Love.*

of the Protestant Reformers, particularly Calvin, as well as in the writings of John Wesley. It is through the work of the Holy Spirit that we are united to Christ so as to participate in his humanity and in the intimacy of the Father-Son relationship.[26] This participation is twofold: we participate in Christ's death ("You have died and your life is hidden with Christ in God" [Col. 3:3]) and in his ongoing resurrected life ("I have been crucified with Christ, and it is no longer I who live, but Christ lives in me. So the life I now live in the body, I live because of the faithfulness of the Son of God" [Gal. 2:20]). In recent decades, New Testament scholars have recognized what the early church fathers also saw: participation in Christ's death and life is in the foreground of New Testament teaching about the death and resurrection of Christ; atonement for transgressions, while important, is in the background. To put it another way: the New Testament focus is on the ongoing personal relationship established by the person and work of Christ, rather than on the atonement as expiation for sins. As E. P. Sanders has written:

> The *prime significance* which the death of Christ has for Paul is not that it provides atonement for past transgressions (although he holds the common Christian view that it does so) but that, by *sharing* in Christ's death one dies to the *power* of sin or to the old aeon, with the result that one *belongs to God*. . . . This transfer takes place by *participation* in Christ's death. . . . One participates in salvation by becoming one person with Christ, dying with him to sin and sharing the promise of his resurrection.[27]

This participation is accomplished through the work of the Holy Spirit. "It is still in the name of Jesus Christ that the Holy Spirit comes to us, and no other name."[28]

---

26. Douglas Fairbairn, *Introduction to Theology* (Downers Grove, IL: InterVarsity Press, 2009), loc. 3278, Kindle ed.

27. E. P. Sanders, *Paul and Palestinian Judaism: A Comparison of Patterns of Religion* (Minneapolis: Fortress, 1977), 467–68, 549. Italics added to "prime significance."

28. Thomas F. Torrance, *Theology in Reconstruction* (Grand Rapids: Eerdmans, 1965), 247.

Pope John Paul II writes, "Man is called to a fullness of life which far exceeds the dimensions of earthly existence, because it consists in sharing the very life of God."[29]

Theosis

The term *theosis*, or "deification,"[30] is one that strikes our Protestant ears as very strange. But this was the category used by the ancient church to speak of salvation. Sometimes when I have introduced statements like that of Athanasius, who said of Christ, "he became man that we might become gods," students have asked me, "Were these guys Mormons?" The answer of course is, "No." The terminology reflects, however inadequately, the biblical concept of our participation in the very life of God. It is a reality explicitly affirmed by the apostle Peter (2 Peter 1:4).[31]

Likewise *theosis* is not pantheism, whether of the popular Western version (as seen in Shirley McClain's *Out on a Limb*, where she proclaims, "I am God") or the thoroughly Eastern one, according to which we are absorbed into the divine through a mystical experience and our

---

29. Pope John Paul II, *The Gospel of Life* (New York: Random House, 1995), 4.

30. "Deification" comes from the Latin translation of the Greek term *theosis*. Unfortunately, the Latin and English terms suggest a becoming, in the sense of a transformation of natures. This is not implied by the Greek term *theosis*, which speaks of sharing in the divine nature rather than a transformation whereby the believer becomes divine. Below is a definition of *theosis* given at http://orthodoxwiki.org:

> Theosis ("deification," "divinization") is the process of a worshiper becoming free of *hamartía* ("missing the mark"), being united with God, beginning in this life and later consummated in bodily resurrection. For Orthodox Christians, *théōsis* (see 2 Peter 1:4) is salvation. *Théōsis* assumes that humans from the beginning are made to share in the Life or Nature of the all. Therefore, an infant or an adult worshiper is saved from the state of unholiness (*hamartia*—which is not to be confused with *hamártēma* "sin") for participation in the Life (*zōé*, not simply *bíos*) of the Trinity—which is everlasting. This is not to be confused with the heretical *apothéōsis*—'Deification in God's Essence,' which is imparticipable.

31. The New English Translation notes: "Although the author has borrowed the expression *partakers of the divine nature* from paganism, his meaning is clearly Christian. He does not mean apotheosis (man becoming a god) in the pagan sense, but rather that believers have an organic connection with God. Because of such a connection, God can truly be called our Father. Conceptually, this bears the same meaning as Paul's 'in Christ' formula. The author's statement, though startling at first, is hardly different from Paul's prayer for the Ephesians that they 'may be filled up to all the fullness of God' (3:19)."

personhood disappears into the greater being of The One (impersonal god). Rather, *participation* involves us creatures becoming united with Christ while retaining our individual identities. We are adopted into the divine family. We are brought in by the unfathomable grace and love of God, who has sacrificed himself on our behalf in the person of his Son and has called us, as his adopted children, to participate in the joy of divine life. *Theosis* speaks graphically of the transformation of our fallen human existence into a redeemed existence that participates in the very life of the triune God—or, as other theologians have said, of our becoming participants in the great dance of divine life.

As Protestants, when we hear the term "salvation" our minds immediately go to the reality of justification by faith. In other words, we view salvation in the static legal categories of forgiveness of sin and acquittal, of the judge declaring us not guilty and not liable for the penalty of sin any longer. One of the great weaknesses in Protestantism is that we have viewed salvation *solely* in these terms, as justification by faith and nothing more. We have forgotten that the point of salvation is not just to stay out of hell, but to be joined with God in an eternal participation in the divine life; it is relational. In fact, a dominant scriptural image for salvation is marriage, which is by definition relational. As the *Westminster Shorter Catechism* question 1 states, "the chief end of man is to glorify God and *enjoy him forever.*" That participation is spoken of throughout the New Testament in terms of our being *in Christ* (*en Christō*).

The theological terminology for this is "union with Christ." As the apostle Peter says, we "become partakers of the divine nature" (2 Peter 1:4). It is the work of the Spirit to effect this personal union with God as Trinity, and through that union to transform us progressively. It is the Spirit who forms us, progressively working in us to make this union effective in our lives; he is the agent of growth. It is not our work but that of the Spirit dwelling in us that is "leading us to union—to transforming, personal, intimate relationship with the triune God."[32] In the words of Jesus himself, "This is eternal life: that they may *know*[33] you, the only true God, and Jesus Christ whom you have sent" (John 17:3). Jesus prays "that

---

32. Pinnock, *The Flame of Love*, 149.

33. The term for "know" used here is *ginōskō*, which denotes experiential knowledge, rather than *oida*, which speaks of intellectual knowledge.

the love with which you have loved me may be in them, and I in them" (17:26). Our home is with the triune God. As the psalmist says, "LORD, you have been our dwelling place in all generations" (Ps. 90:1).

Even the term "atonement," which is used only once in the King James Version of the New Testament, literally means "at-one-ment" and is therefore usually rendered "reconciliation" (as in Rom. 5:11). To our ears the term atonement is inexorably bound up with Jesus' sacrificial death on the cross for the expiation of sins, yet the term in itself actually stands for more: oneness or unity between God and humanity, the "loving relationality into which the Spirit is drawing people. The Spirit is bringing us into intimacy with the Father through the Son, who is sharing his divine sonship with us."[34]

Paul tells us that the love of God has been poured out through the Holy Spirit in our hearts (Rom. 5:5). It is the presence of the Holy Spirit, not an act apart from the Spirit, that is the basis of the love of God in our hearts. Further, I would suggest that this "love of God" is not our love for God, but rather his love for us. As the apostle John says, "we love him because he first loved us" (1 John 4:19). The *objective* proof of God's love for us is his giving himself to us in the incarnation: God in unfathomable humility and self-denial became one of his creatures. The climax of this self-giving love of God is found in Christ the God-man on the cross. The *subjective* proof of his love for us is the presence of the Holy Spirit within us, "the Lord and giver of life," whose temple we have become individually and corporately.[35]

Salvation is more than a paid-up fire insurance policy. It is more than a change in legal status. It is an ongoing mutual embrace between each of us and the triune God who is love itself. The medieval mystic Bernard of Clairvaux eloquently expressed this in a sermon on the Song of Songs: "If the Father kisses the Son and the Son receives the kiss, it is appropriate to think of the Holy Spirit as the kiss."[36] Through the work of the Spirit within us we have been drawn into this eternal dance of love.

---

34. John Paul II, *The Gospel of Life*, 4.

35. See 1 Corinthians 3:16–17 and 6:19–20.

36. Bernard of Clairvaux, "Holy Spirit: Kiss of the Mouth," in *Selected Writings*, ed. and trans. G. R. Evans (New York: Paulist, 1987), 237.

C. S. Lewis speaks of the inconsolable longing within us,[37] a longing that meets us unexpectedly through experiences that open up a momentary vision of eternal realities. These fleeting glimpses awaken in our hearts the desire for something more. But the something more is not to be found in the experience itself, and if we try to re-create the experience that awoke the transcendent longing, we will fail to connect with it.[38] It cannot be invoked at will, but is given to us from a source outside ourselves. Some authors have identified the source of this inconsolable longing as the work of the Spirit as he effects *theosis* within us.

Clark Pinnock does not overstate the case when he observes: "Salvation is the Spirit, who indwells us, drawing us toward participation in the life of the triune God. The goal is union with God at the marriage supper of the Lamb."[39] To this end Jesus prays, "Father, I desire that those also, whom you have given me, may be with me where I am, to see my glory, which you have given me because you loved me before the foundation of the world" (John 17:24).

God intends our life here on earth as Christians to be one elevated to full participation in the life of God. The process begins here and now in the midst of our existence in this fallen world; it is in this world that we begin to experience the presence of God with us. Scripture employs many images to convey the reality that our true identity is found in our participation in the life of the triune God through the Spirit: we are sons of God, joint-heirs with Christ (Rom. 8:17); our life is hidden with Christ in God (Col. 3:3). It is in God that we live and move and have our being (Acts 17:28). We are indwelt by the Holy Spirit; Christ dwells in our hearts by faith. The Spirit sweeps us up into the love of God, so that walking in the Spirit we become ever better acquainted with the love that surpasses knowledge, and are filled with the divine fullness (Eph. 3:16–19). The Spirit summons us to a transforming friendship with God that leads to sharing in the triune life.

Again, this transformation, this participation, this *theosis*, is a work of God the Holy Spirit; it is most emphatically not our work. Paul tells

---

37. C. S. Lewis, *Surprised by Joy* (New York: Harcourt Brace Jovanovich, 1955), 74.

38. We might compare this to the way into Lewis's Narnia: every time the children enter this magical land, it is through a different door.

39. Pinnock, *The Flame of Love*, 150.

us that all those led by the Spirit of God are the sons of God (Rom. 8:14). We do cooperate in the Spirit's work, but our doing so is like the relationship of dance partners on the ballroom floor. The Spirit leads us, but he does not drag us kicking and screaming, nor does he say, "Get in line and follow my footsteps!" Rather, he exerts that gentle, loving, barely perceptible pressure that is communicated in dance and through which the two partners function as one, in sync. In line with this imagery, J. I. Packer speaks of "keeping in step"[40] with the Spirit, while Bill Hybels speaks of "the power of a whisper."[41] Elijah in his fear and exhaustion found God not in the earthquake or wind or fire, but in a "still small voice" (1 Kings 19:12).

This brings up another important point. Paul tells us that the fruit of the Spirit is love, joy, peace, patience, kindness, goodness, faithfulness, gentleness, and self-control (Gal. 5:22–23). Throughout my life I have heard many speakers talk about the need to cultivate these characteristics in our lives. I have heard them cite strategies such as focusing one day on being loving, the next day on being joyful, the next day on feeling peaceful, and so on. Such advice in fact totally misses the point and throws us back on our own resources as opposed to participating in the work of the Spirit.

In presenting the fruit of the Spirit, Paul is drawing a double contrast. The first is between Spirit and "flesh"—frail human life lived apart from participation with and empowerment by the Spirit. The second is between fruit and works or deeds. Deeds are activities that are consciously chosen, while fruit is a direct and natural product of life. A tree does not decide to bear fruit; it does not struggle to bear fruit. Rather, fruit is the natural byproduct of the tree's healthy life. Likewise spiritual fruit—love, joy, peace, and so on—is the byproduct of our participation in the divine life. To set out a method for trying to produce the fruit of the Spirit by willpower is simply to feed what Richard Lovelace has described as the "religious flesh."[42] The product may look good on the

---

40. J. I. Packer, *Keep in Step with the Spirit: Finding Fullness in Our Walk with God* (Grand Rapids: Revell, 1987).

41. Bill Hybels, *The Power of a Whisper: Hearing God, Having the Guts to Respond* (Grand Rapids: Zondervan, 2012).

42. Richard Lovelace, *The Dynamics of Spiritual Life* (Downers Grove, IL: InterVarsity Press, 1979), 95–144, esp. 102–104.

surface, but when the skin is peeled back it is filled with pride and self-righteousness.

To take this a step further, I would argue that there is actually only one fruit of the Spirit: love! Significantly, if we compare the characteristics of love listed by Paul in 1 Corinthians 13 with the list of the fruit of the Spirit in Galatians 5, there is a startling correlation. What I'm saying here is that the fruit of the Spirit is love because that Spirit is God himself, who is love itself. The joy, peace, patience, kindness, goodness, and so on are all characteristics of love; they are what love looks like in action in various situations. Additionally, these lists are representative, not exhaustive. Jesus told the disciples in no uncertain terms, "By this shall all men know that you are my disciples, by the fact that you love one another" (John 13:35)—not that you are religious, not that you are ethical, not even that you do good deeds, but "that you love one another"!

The breadth of the Spirit's activities is cosmic. The Spirit is the "point man" of the triune God's presence on earth, and his activities are a concrete illustration of the universality of God's grace. Paul makes this very clear in Acts 17 as he preaches on Mars Hill about the creator who loves his creation and all that is in it. God's ongoing love and care for the world is effected by the Spirit. He is "the hope of all the ends of the earth and of the farthest seas" (Ps. 65:5). He is the reconciler of the whole world (2 Cor. 5:19). A rainbow of mercy encircles his throne (Rev. 4:2–3). God's mercies do not fail (Lam. 3:22); his generosity is inexhaustible. Let no one limit his liberality or begrudge its extent (Matt. 20:15). This is central to the Christian worldview and the proclamation of the good news. It is we who so often mistakenly divide life into the spiritual and secular; the Scriptures present no such distinction. "The Spirit meets people not only in religious spheres but everywhere—in the natural world, in the give-and-take of relationships, in the systems that structure human life. No nook or cranny is untouched by the finger of God. His warm breath streams toward humanity with energy and life."[43] As the creed says, the Spirit is "the Lord and giver of life."

---

43. Pinnock, *The Flame of Love*, 150.

Conclusion

As I noted in the introduction, some time ago I was teaching a one-night seminar on the Trinity at a local church, tracing the trajectory of the development of the doctrine of the Trinity from the time of the New Testament to the Council of Nicaea. About halfway through the presentation I was interrupted by one of the attendees who objected to the whole discussion on the Trinity and my implicit assumption that the doctrine of the Trinity was rational. This individual, now in his eighties, is a conservative evangelical out of a fundamentalist background who has a Ph.D. in theology, and yet he holds the Trinity to be fundamentally irrational. In his objection he echoed Thomas Jefferson's complaint about bad Trinitarian math, that 1+1+1=1. He also invoked the logical "law of non-contradiction," which states that contradictory statements cannot both be true at the same time in the same way, contending that Trinitarian explanations violate the law of non-contradiction and are therefore inherently irrational. Surprisingly, he did not insist that the doctrine of the Trinity was untrue, but that we should not waste time trying to understand it because of its inherent irrationality.

This episode graphically drove home to me the poverty of our Western understanding of the Trinity, an understanding that confines *the fundamental Christian assertion of the divine identity* to the uncharted area of "mystery," to be believed but not understood on any level. As noted previously, underlying this thinking is an inherent dualism with roots in ancient Greek philosophy rather than holistic Hebraic thinking rooted in the categories revealed by God in the Old Testament.

Despite the popular (mis)understanding, the historic testimony of the church is that God as he is in himself can be truly *apprehended*, though not fully *comprehended*. I have maintained the same throughout this book. But in order to apprehend God correctly *we must submit our rational faculties to God as he has revealed himself to be,* and not subject his self-revelation to philosophical and epistemological categories of thought that we bring *a priori* to the table. We have subjected divine revelation to hermeneutical lenses that have warped our view of reality. The consequence, for all practical purposes, is that Western Christianity has lost any appreciation of the significance of the Trinity, and in the process driven a wedge between the Father and the Son. Jesus is accorded the status of Son of God, but is popularly regarded as different in character or nature from God himself, thus breaking the eternal unity of the Son with the Father. In this understanding we are truly cut off from the heart of the Father.

We subject God to our preconceptions because we have never been taught to recognize that we necessarily view reality through interpretive lenses. These lenses, whose existence we tend to ignore if not deny outright, must be taken off and reground to allow us to see clearly. Rahner has not overstated the case: as Western Christians we live our lives as "mere monotheists."[1] In so doing we have from a practical perspective unwittingly forfeited the benefits of a relationship of love offered by the Father, Son, and Spirit, and remained enslaved to fear of condemnation.

Our default understandings cause us to create, in the words of Athanasius, mythological deities. These mythological theological projections have driven a wedge in our understanding between the Father and the Son and resulted in us losing the reality of the Trinity. While we verbally acknowledge that Jesus is the Son of God, we fail to recognize his full equality with the Father. In so doing, the eternal unity of the Son with the Father is compromised. Moreover, the effect of this wedge is to *cut us off from any true knowledge of the Father* because despite Jesus' own testimony we do not believe that to see Jesus is to see the Father. In our understanding, Jesus and the Father are not truly one; Jesus has not given us a true glimpse of the Father's love and his desire for us to engage in intimate communion with him as his adopted children through Jesus. These misunderstandings hamper our spiritual lives.

While God gave the Torah to Israel, this revelation was not a personal revelation of God himself in the sense we have been discussing, but instruction from God to mold Israel into the "womb of the

---

1. Karl Rahner, *The Trinity* (New York: Crossroad, 2005), 10–11.

incarnation."[2] It was instruction expressly intended to prepare Israel with the necessary concepts in order that, at the appointed time, they might recognize Jesus for who he was and is. From its beginning the fathers of the church fastened on Matthew 11:27 ("No one knows the Father but the Son. No one knows the Son but the Father and those to whom he chooses to reveal him") to insist that there was a closed loop of knowing between the Father and the Son:[3] God the Father could not be known apart from the Son. Knowledge of God comes only through the incarnate Christ who is one with the Father. The Pharisees thought that knowledge of the Scriptures brought salvation, but they missed the point—the Scriptures pointed to Jesus, the incarnate eternal Son of the Father! It was *he* who was Immanuel, *God with us.* This same conclusion of the Pharisees about the Scriptures is, I believe, dangerously woven into the warp and woof of fundamentalism and evangelicalism.

During Second Temple Judaism, even the Jews in Palestine succumbed to the influence of Hellenistic philosophy. In fact, many scholars have recognized that Phariseeism itself embodied the Hellenization of Judaism. Coincidentally, and for different reasons, during this era the position of God was confined to one of utter transcendence, so that the possibility of any knowledge of God as he existed in himself was denied. He was totally incomprehensible. During this time "the God of the Old Testament Scriptures, the God of Judaism, seems to have become something of a negative border-line concept."[4]

The knowledge of God in the Old Testament revelation, as it came to be understood and interpreted in the Jewish tradition over time, did not have theological content in the strictly abstract sense of the term. God

---

2. See Thomas F. Torrance, *The Mediation of Christ* (Colorado Springs, CO: Helmers & Howard, 1992), 18-19.

3. Jeremias notes of Matthew 11:27: "'My father has given me all things.' Matthew 28.18 should not mislead us into supposing that πάντα ["all things"] refers to lordly power; this would not fit the context of vv. 25f. and 27 b–d, where only the revelation of God is mentioned. As παραδιδόναι (= רסמ, [translated "has given"]) is used as a technical term for the transmission of doctrine, knowledge and holy lore, πάντα ["all things"] refers to knowledge of God, just as ταῦτα ["these things"] in v. 25 designates the mystery of revelation. Thus in v. 25a, Jesus is saying: God has given me a full revelation" (Joachim Jeremias, The Prayers of Jesus [Philadelphia: Fortress, 1989], 49).

4. Thomas F. Torrance, *The Mediation of Christ* (Colorado Springs, CO: Helmers and Howard, 1992), 120. The following discussion is summarized from pp. 119–26.

in himself was understood to be unknowable undifferentiated unity; he could be known only through his concrete actions toward Israel as his covenant people, as well as his control of the world. While he could be recognized as "incorporeal, eternal and omnipotent, [and] characterized by kindness, goodness, justice, holiness and perfection,"[5] any hint that he could be known as he existed within his transcendent being was simply impossible. Some even claimed that YHWH was not only beyond knowing, he was even beyond virtue. This view of God is close to the Neoplatonic conception of God that has plagued the Western church at least since the early Middle Ages.

After the destruction of the Temple in AD 70, Rabbinic Judaism settled on a purely negative approach to knowing God (*apophatic*, i.e., saying what he is not rather than what he is). This understanding of who God is precluded any kind of personal knowledge of him or any I-Thou relationship with him.

But the early church rejected this approach, and understood that in the person of Jesus, God had come to us as Immanuel, God with us. Jesus was God by virtue of the fact that he was the creator of all as well as the continuing ruler of all. The church recognized that YHWH, the eternal creator and God of Israel, had "earthed" himself in human form in a way that no one could have expected. God himself had become one of us. Jesus was the concrete historical manifestation of the eternal Son of the Father in human flesh.

The church of the fourth century, the Nicene era, formally recognized that God was Trinity, but that Trinitarian existence had two components: the "immanent Trinity" (often called the "ontological Trinity"), or God in his eternal being, and the "economic Trinity," God in his personal relations with the creation. The key term of the Nicene Creed, *homoousios*, provided the link, the "ontological connection between the economic Trinity and the immanent Trinity," applying not just to the external or economic "relations of the Son and the Spirit to the Father but to inner relations of the Trinity as a whole."[6]

The patristic fathers insisted that God's *being* was in his *act* (of revelation); during the Reformation, the Reformers stressed that the *act* of

---

5. Ibid.
6. Ibid., 123.

God is in his *being*. In the past century, several theologians have insisted that both perspectives are true and must be held together: God's act is in his being and his being is in his act. While this is a bit difficult to grasp, it is an important concept as it applies to Trinitarian understanding. As Thomas Torrance explains it, "what God is toward us in his revealing and saving acts as Father, Son and Holy Spirit, he is antecedently and eternally in himself, but also . . . what God is antecedently and eternally in himself as Father, Son and Holy Spirit he is toward us in his revealing and saving acts in Christ and in the Holy Spirit."[7] In other words, with God "what you see is what you get." There is no hidden agenda; there are no dark secrets. There is no wedge between the Father and the Son. Specifically, what you see in Jesus is exactly who God is in his inner being. As Jesus himself said, "Whoever has seen me has seen the Father" (John 14:9).

This truth is vital. In order for salvation to be accomplished there had to be an unbroken continuity of divine presence and activity between the Father and Christ. Were this not the case, the person of Christ would become irrelevant for salvation. Only God can forgive sins. Unless Christ is fully God in the same sense that the Father is God, while at the same time fully sharing our humanity, his death on the cross might be seen as a grand gesture, but it could not provide salvation for humanity.

The same is true for the Holy Spirit: the same unbroken continuity of divine presence and activity between the Father and the Spirit is required, or his activity is void of salvific significance for us. As Thomas Torrance has observed:

> The Holy Spirit is the transcendent freedom of God to be present to us in such a way as to realise our relationship with God as the creative and sustaining Source of our being and life. He is the sanctifying, life-giving and redeeming outreach of God toward us, drawing us into communion with himself, undergirding that in the form of a relation of God to himself, for he is not only God coming to us but God dwelling in us and upholding us from below in a saving communion with himself. In

---

7. Ibid., 124.

him God gives us nothing less than himself: in him the divine
Gift and the divine Giver are identical.[8]

The perichoretic union of the divine persons, their mutual indwelling
of one another, their dynamic giving and receiving of love in relationship, is what constitutes the Trinity.[9] In this mutual indwelling they
are completely one. No member of the Trinity is properly himself apart
from the other two. "This triune relation between the Father, the Son
and the Holy Spirit applies to all their activity, not least in the movement of atoning propitiation and expiation whereby all who come to
the Father through the Son and in the Holy Spirit are redeemed and
saved from sin and death and judgment."[10] The doctrine of the Trinity
is not only about God as he is in his inner being and relations, which we
grasp as abstract facts to file in our mental filing cabinets; it points to
a dynamic reality that is the very heart of the gospel, grounded in and
springing forth from the heart of God. It is profoundly existential and
life-transforming as we grasp that reality of which it speaks.

Grasped at a heart level, the unity of the Trinity transforms the fundamental basis of our theological understanding and spiritual lives. It
controls the way we think and speak of all theological and spiritual
realities.

---

8. Ibid., 125.

9. John D. Zizioulas, *Being as Communion* (New York: St. Vladimir's Seminary
Press, 1985), 44–46.

10. Thomas F. Torrance, *The Mediation of Christ*, 126.

He, She, or It? Gender and the Holy Spirit

The issue of how we properly refer to the Spirit, quietly pondered in the background by scholars for centuries, has been brought into the forefront recently by William Paul Young in his work *The Shack*. Breaking convention, Young portrayed the Holy Spirit as female, embodied, and having a name, Sarayu (a Hindi word for "wind"). Honoring Young's insights into the Spirit, C. Baxter Kruger followed his example and referred to the Spirit as "she" in his follow-up theological reflection on *The Shack* titled *The Shack Revisited*.

As noted earlier, it is difficult to construct a doctrine of the Holy Spirit given that the Spirit is presented existentially in Scripture and that much of the Spirit's activity is universal and immanent in the world. Even reference to the Spirit is awkward. In Western Christianity, male terminology has historically been used to refer to the Spirit. But the question of how to refer to the Spirit is not a simple one in contemporary society. This is not because God or the Spirit has changed, but because theological language is necessarily analogical; it communicates concepts by way of analogy. The principle of analogy has been formally acknowledged since Thomas Aquinas wrote on it in the thirteenth century, although it was informally recognized even in the early church.

The Greek language has terms for humanity that are gender-specif-ic—*anēr* ("male," "man") and *gunaika* ("female," "woman")—as well as terms that embrace both genders, such as *anthropos* ("human being"). Likewise German uses *Mann* to refer to the male of the species and *Frau* to speak of the female, while *Mensch* refers to both genders. The English language does not contain vocabulary that is unambiguously gender-neutral while at the same time personal. Historically, it had only one word, "man," to refer either to the male of the species or to a human being whether male or female, but the latter use has now lost most of its currency. Meanwhile, the rise of feminism during the past generation has raised the issue of gender in relation to the way we think of God. The charge has been that the dominantly male language employed in English reduces women to second-class citizens in society and in the kingdom of God.

Such assertions notwithstanding, there is a general recognition that assigning sexual function to God is a reversion to the pagan concep-tions of the ancient Canaanite deities who were regularly involved in sexual functions that brought fertility to the land. As Mary Hayter has observed: "Today a growing number of feminists teach that the God/ess combines male and female characteristics. They, like those who assume God is exclusively male, should remember that any attribution of sexuality to God is a reversion to paganism."[11] But simply to refer to God in a gendered way is not reversion into paganism (otherwise English-speakers would be doomed to paganism), nor is it necessary to avoid any reference to male and female roles to communicate the idea that God is neither male nor female. As Wolfhart Pannenberg has noted:

> The aspect of fatherly care in particular is taken over in what the Old Testament has to say about God's fatherly concern for Israel. The sexual definition of the father's role plays no part. . . . To bring sexual differentiation into the understanding of God would mean polytheism; it was thus ruled out for the God of Israel. . . . The fact that God's care for Israel can also be

---

11. Mary Hayter, *New Even in Christ* (London: SPCK, 1983), n.p. Cited by Alister McGrath in *Christian Theology: An Introduction* (Oxford: Blackwell, 2001), 286.

expressed in terms of a mother's love shows clearly enough how little there is any sense of sexual distinction in the understanding of God as Father.[12]

As far as gendered reference to God is concerned, the first person of the godhead is referred to properly as "Father," if for no other reason than Jesus' example and command to his disciples as to the proper form of address to use when praying. As the term is used of humans, a father is by definition male.[13] The second person of the Trinity was incarnated as a male and is thus appropriately referred to as male in his incarnate form. Note that both "Father" and "Jesus" are personal terms. The issues of reference to the Spirit, however, are more problematic, from both a linguistic and a historical perspective.

From the earliest Christian centuries in some parts of the church the Spirit was pictured in female terms. This imagery is implicit in the New Testament itself. Believers are "born of" the Holy Spirit, and the Spirit is the "mother" of God's children. The Spirit is also the *Paraclete* ("comforter") who comforts "as a mother comforts her children" (Isa. 66:13).

While the church in the Latin West staunchly opposed feminine references to God, the church of the East embraced such language, particularly with reference to the Holy Spirit. Feminine references to the Spirit stem from the early second century. Aphraates, a fourth-century Syrian monk, bishop, and ascetic, unabashedly spoke of the Holy Spirit as mother: "Why does a man forsake father and mother when he takes a wife? This is the explanation: as long as a man has no wife, he loves and reverences God his Father and the Holy Spirit his Mother, and has no other love."[14] Likewise Symeon of Mesopotamia wrote a series of sermons that speak of the "motherly" ministry of the Holy Spirit. He used two arguments to establish his claim:

---

12. Wolfhart Pannenberg, *Systematic Theology I* (Grand Rapids: Eerdmans, 1991), 260–61.

13. Interestingly, however, Young defies not only theological but linguistic convention here: he gives the masculine name "Papa"—intimate form of "Father"—to the character representing the first person of the Trinity, but the character is female and is referred to by feminine pronouns.

14. Jürgen Moltmann, *The Spirit of Life: A Universal Affirmation* (Minneapolis: Fortress, 2001), 158.

1. The promised Comforter (the Paraclete) will "comfort you as a mother comforts" (here John 14.26 is put together with Isa. 66.13); and 2. Only the person who has been "born anew" can see the kingdom of God. Men and women are "born anew" from the Spirit. They are "children of the Spirit" and the Spirit is their "Mother."[15]

These works were translated into German in the seventeenth century, influencing the emerging Pietist movement leaders August Hermann Franke and Count Nicholas von Zinzendorf as well as the Moravian Brethren. Among the Moravians this emphasis produced a community-centered mentality; as Jürgen Moltmann notes, "a certain de-patriarchalization of the picture of God results in a de-patriarchalization and de-hierarchalization of the church too."[16] He further observes:

> Giving birth, nourishing, protecting and consoling, love's empathy and sympathy: these are then the expressions which suggest themselves as a way of describing the relations of the Spirit to her children. They express mutual intimacy, not sovereign and aweful distance.[17]

Likewise contemporary Anabaptist theologian Thomas Finger focuses on the motherly images of the Spirit in Scripture: "The Spirit comforts, encourages, yearns and brings to birth. Most of her activities are best expressed in feminine terminology."[18]

As a language, English has natural grammatical gender for referents that reflect the physical anatomy of animate beings, whether human or animal, with all other objects referred to as neuter or genderless: "it" as opposed to "he" or "she." This is a general, not an absolute, rule: ships are referred to as feminine, while boats are referred to as neuter. Many other languages, including Greek, are more highly inflected and

---

15. Ibid.
16. Ibid., 160.
17. Ibid., 159.
18. Thomas N. Finger, *Christian Theology: An Eschatological Approach* (Scottdale, PA: Herald, 1987), 2:486, cited by Clark Pinnock in *The Flame of Love* (Downers Grove, IL: InterVarsity Press, 1999), 235.

include nouns that are masculine, feminine, and neuter, with apparently arbitrary assignment of words to a particular grammatical gender. For example, in Greek the words for "son" and "daughter" are grammatically masculine and feminine respectively, while the word for "child" is neuter. Hebrew, like Greek, is also highly inflected, with an equally arbitrary assignment of nouns to either of only two genders, masculine or feminine. One standard introductory Hebrew grammar explains it this way:

> Nearly all Hebrew nouns belong to one of two grammatical categories called gender: masculine and feminine. Nouns denoting animate beings usually have grammatical gender corresponding to natural gender (sex), but there is otherwise no clear correlation between gender and meaning. For example *har* (mountain) is masculine, while *gib'ah* (hill) is feminine.[19]

Linguistically the Greek term used in the New Testament for S/ spirit, *pneuma*, is neuter, as is the English "spirit." In the Greek New Testament the Spirit is only occasionally spoken of in masculine terms, the significant exception being the Gospel of John: John uses the masculine pronoun, but only when speaking of the Spirit as the "Paraclete" because the word *parakletos* is masculine. The problem in English is that the neuter pronoun "it" is impersonal; the only way to avoid using a gendered pronoun is to use an impersonal pronoun. To follow grammatical rules by referring to the Holy Spirit as "it" is surely improper, if for no other reason than that the narrative of Acts clearly presents the Spirit in personal terms, as do Paul's epistles.

Recent studies have pointed out that in the Hebrew Old Testament the use of the word for "spirit," *ruach*, is predominantly grammatically feminine. Of the 84 times the term is used with reference to the Spirit of God in the Hebrew text, its feminine form is used 75 times. The 9 remaining uses are masculine. In 40 of these 75 feminine usages, the accompanying verbs are also in the feminine form.

From this linguistic data R. P. Nettlehorst draws a radical conclusion:

---

19. Thomas O. Lambdin, *Introduction to Biblical Hebrew* (New York: Charles Scribner's Sons, 1971), 3.

Our traditional assumption of a masculine Spirit is questionable; in fact, the evidence seems overwhelming that the Spirit
should be viewed as "She," which does seem to make sense, since
the other two members of the godhead are labeled "Father" and
"Son."[20]

Such a radical conclusion strikes me as going far beyond the evidence.
The evidence for this conclusion is not "overwhelming." As noted above,

---

20. R. P. Nettelhorst, "More Than Just a Controversy: All about the Holy Spirit,"
Quartz Hill Journal of Theology 3, no. 1 (http://theology.edu/journal/volume3/spirit.
htm). Nettlehorst draws four implications from this use of the feminine *ruach* in the
Old Testament:

A feminine Holy Spirit clarifies how women can also be said to be created in the
"image of God." It has long been recognized that the Godhead must include some
feminine aspects since Genesis 1:26–27 explicitly states that both men and women
were created in God's image.

A feminine Holy Spirit explains the identity of the personified wisdom in Proverbs
8:12–31.

The third benefit of recognizing the femininity of the Holy Spirit is that it explains
the subservient role that the Spirit plays. The Bible seems to indicate that the Spirit
does not speak for itself or about itself; rather the Spirit only speaks what it hears. The
Spirit is said to have come into the world to glorify Christ (see John 16:13–14; Acts
13:2). In contrast, it should be noted that Scripture represents both the Father and the
Son speaking from and of themselves.

Finally, a feminine Holy Spirit, with a Father and a Son as the rest of the Trinity,
may help explain why the family is the basic unit of human society.

These implications from Nettlehorst deserve comment. The so-called clarification
falls into the error of confusing aspects of the economic Trinity (the "job descriptions"
of the individual persons of the Trinity in relation to the creation) with the ontological
or immanent Trinity (the eternal intra-Trinitarian personal relationship). While
it is popular to invoke "Rahner's Rule" (that the economic Trinity is the immanent
Trinity), there are limitations to its application, as Thomas F. Torrance has pointed out.
Certainly the femininity of the Spirit is not an unambiguous revelation of Scripture.
It is perhaps *at best* a plausible inference, and as an inference it must be treated with
great care. The second inference is possible, but again highly speculative and cutting
against two millennia of interpretation. This does not make it wrong, but the onus
of demonstration is on the author to demonstrate the viability of this interpretation,
which he has not done. The third implication rests on assumptions about hierarchy and
male headship that violate the most basic Christian assertion about the Trinity, the
homoousion and the concept of *perichoresis*. The fourth implication, regarding family,
reflects faint echoes of the concept of community developed by the Pietists, which,
when implemented, had the effect of *de*-patriarchalization and *de*-hierarchalization.
This is the exact opposite of the effect that Nettlehorst seems to be implicitly endorsing.

grammatical gender in a language is apparently often an arbitrary thing. It is reading far too much into a grammatical feature of the Hebrew language to draw a hard and fast conclusion based on that feature alone.

More cautious theologians and exegetes have not jumped on the Spirit-feminizing bandwagon. Even Clark Pinnock, who sees formidable evidence for a "feminine side" of the Holy Spirit and expresses a desire to refer to the Spirit in feminine terminology, nonetheless recognizes the objections and nuances his conclusion: John speaks of the Spirit as masculine. No appeal to the use of the feminine gender in Hebrew can get around this. Likewise, to speak of the Holy Spirit in exclusively feminine terms would effectively negate masculine imagery used of the Spirit as well as downplay the feminine imagery used of the Father and the Son. Certainly it is improper to *contrast* the femininity of the Spirit with the non-femininity of the Father and the Son. Indeed, it is the Spirit who is the agent of conception in the Virgin Mary (very much a male function when viewed from the perspective of gendered imagery).[21]

New Testament scholar Gordon Fee observes, in speaking of the difficulty in using pronouns for God, "In view of the lack of pronouns for God I follow the historic practice of using the masculine pronouns; but I do not for a minute think that God is male (or female). God is God, and includes in himself all that is essential to our being male and female, while at the same time transcending such distinctions."[22]

To return to the original question: how should we refer to the Spirit? Understanding that theological language is analogical (that is, based on analogy) as opposed to univocal (having only one possible meaning), and given the variety of images used for the Spirit, images that encompass both female and male roles, it seems appropriate to leave this question open. Whatever terminology is adopted must be personal since the Spirit is without question presented as a personal and relational presence in Scripture. The data from Scripture and from usage throughout the history of the church suggests that it is permissible to use either gender with reference to the Spirit while at the same time being careful

---

21. Pinnock, *The Flame of Love*, 17.
22. Gordon Fee, *God's Empowering Presence* (Peabody, MA: Hendrickson, 1994), xxiii.

not to make such use (or the use of any gendered or relational language referring to the Trinity) a basis for teaching or enforcing a hierarchical understanding of intra-Trinitarian relationships. Such would be a violation of the church's most ancient and basic Trinitarian commitments: the *homoousion* and the concept of *perichoresis*.

Bibliography

Anatolios, Khaled. *Retrieving Nicaea: The Development and Meaning of Trinitarian Doctrine*. Grand Rapids: Baker, 2011.

Athanasius. *The Treatise De Incarnatione Verbi Dei*. London: A. R. Mowbray, 1953.

Barbour, Ian G. *Issues in Science and Religion*. Englewood Cliffs, NJ: Prentice-Hall, 1966.

Bauckham, Richard. *God Crucified: Monotheism and Christology in the New Testament*. Grand Rapids: Eerdmans, 1999.

Bauman, Michael C. *Pilgrim Theology: Taking the Path of Theological Discovery*. Grand Rapids: Zondervan, 1992.

Bernard of Clairvaux. *Selected Writings*. New York: Paulist, 1987.

Bray, Gerald. *God Is Love: A Biblical and Systematic Theology*. Kindle ed. Wheaton, IL: Crossway, 2012.

———. *The Doctrine of God*. Downers Grove, IL: InterVarsity Press, 1993.

Bromiley, Geoffrey W., ed. and trans. *Theological Dictionary of the New Testament*. Vol. 6. Grand Rapids: Eerdmans, 1968.

Bruner, Frederick, and William Hornden. *The Holy Spirit: The Shy Member of the Trinity*. Eugene, OR: Wipf & Stock, 2001.

Calvin, John. *Institutes of the Christian Religion*. Translated by Ford Lewis Battles. Philadelphia: Westminster, 1977.

Cho, David Yonggi. *The Fourth Dimension: Discovering a New World of Answered Prayer*. Vol. 1. Alachua, FL: Bridge-Logos, 1979.

Clark, Gordon H. *Religion, Reason, and Revelation*. Philadelphia: Presbyterian and Reformed, 1961.

Colyer, Elmer M. *How to Read T. F. Torrance*. Downers Grove, IL: InterVarsity Press, 2001.

Dawson, Garrett Scott, ed. *An Introduction to Torrance Theology: Discovering the Incarnate Savior.* Edinburgh: T & T Clark, 2007.

Del Re, Giuseppe. *The Cosmic Dance: Science Discovers the Mysterious Harmony of the Universe.* Radnor, PA: Templeton Foundation, 2000.

Edwards, Jonathan. *Charity and Its Fruits.* Edinburgh: Banner of Truth, 1982.

Elwell, Walter, ed. *The Evangelical Dictionary of Theology.* 2nd ed. Grand Rapids: Baker, 2001.

Erickson, Millard. *Who's Tampering with the Trinity? An Assessment of the Subordination Debate.* Grand Rapids: Kregel, 2009.

Fairbairn, Douglas. *Life in the Trinity: An Introduction to Theology with the Help of the Church Fathers.* Kindle ed. Downers Grove, IL : InterVarsity Press, 2009.

Fee, Gordon. "Galatians in a Week." Audio series. Vancouver: Regent College, 2005.

Frose, Paul, and Christopher Bader. *America's Four Gods: What We Say about God—And What That Says about Us.* New York: Oxford University Press, 2011.

Giley, Gary. "The Word Faith Movement." n.d. http://www.rapidnet.com/~jbeard/bdm/Psychology/char/more/w-f.htm.

Green, Joel, Scot McKnight, and I. Howard Marshall, eds. *Dictionary of Jesus and the Gospels.* Downers Grove, IL: InterVarsity Press, 2002.

Gunton, Colin. *The Promise of Trinitarian Theology.* New York: T & T Clark, 1997.

———. *The Triune Creator: A Historical and Systematic Study.* Grand Rapids: Eerdmans, 1998.

Hanegraaff, Hank. *Christianity in Crisis: The Twenty-first Century.* Nashville: Thomas Nelson, 2009.

Hilary of Poitiers. "On The Trinity." In *The Nicene and Post-Nicene Fathers,* vol. 9, edited by Philip Schaff. Grand Rapids: Eerdmans, 1975.

Hsu, Al. "He Is Calling for Elijah! Why We Still Mishear Jesus." *Christianity Today,* April 2012. http://www.christianity-today.com/ct/2012/aprilweb-only/my-god-forsaken-me.html?paging=off.

Hufford, Darrin. *The Misunderstood God: The Lies Religion Tells Us about God*. Newberry Park, CA: Windblown Media, 2009.

Irenaeus. "Against Heresies." In *Ante-Nicene Fathers*, vol. 1, edited by Philip Schaff. Garland, TX: Galaxie Software, 2000.

Jefferson, Thomas. *The Writings of Thomas Jefferson*. Edited by H. A. Washington. Washington, DC: Taylor & Maury, 1954. Google Books. http://books.google.com/books?id=kNIcAQAAIAA-J&pg=PA210&lpg=PA210#v=onepage&q&f=false.

Jeremias, Joachim. *The Prayers of Jesus*. London: SCM, 1967.

John Paul II. *The Gospel of Life: Evangelium Vitae*. New York: Pauline Books & Media, 1995.

———. *On the Holy Spirit in the Life of the Church and the World*. New York: St. Paul, 1998.

Johnson, Darrell. *Experiencing the Trinity*. Vancouver: Regent College, 2002.

Kettler, Christian D. *The God Who Believes: Faith, Doubt, and the Vicarious Humanity of Christ*. Eugene, OR: Cascade, 2005.

Kittel, G., ed. *Theological Dictionary of the New Testament*. Vol. 6. Grand Rapids: Eerdmans, 1968.

Kruger, C. Baxter. "Bearing Our Scorn: Jesus and the Way of Trinitarian Love." Perichoresis, 2007. http://perichoresis.org/downloads/BearingOurScorn.pdf.

———. *Jesus and the Undoing of Adam*. Jackson, MS: Perichoresis, 2001.

———. "Rediscovering Jesus." Audio lecture series. Jackson, MS: Perichoresis, 2009.

Leithart, Peter J. *Athanasius*. Grand Rapids: Baker, 2011.

Lewis, C. S. *The Four Loves*. New York: Harcourt Brace Jovanovich, 1960.

———. *Mere Christianity*. New York: Touchstone, 1996.

———. *Surprised by Joy*. New York: Harcourt Brace Jovanovich, 1955.

Losey, Steven. "Is God Like My Dad?" Campus Life, Ignite Your Faith. n.d. http://www.christianitytoday.com/iyf/music/band-sartists/10.34.html.

Lovelace, Richard. *The Dynamics of Spiritual Life: An Evangelical Theology of Renewal*. Downers Grove, IL: InterVarsity Press, 1979.

MacDonald, George. *Creation in Christ: Unspoken Sermons*. Edited by Roland Hein. Vancouver: Regent College, 1976.

Marenbo, John. *Boethius*. New York: Oxford University Press, 2003.

McGrath, Alister. *Reformation Thought: An Introduction*. 3rd ed. Oxford: Blackwell, 1999.

———. *Understanding the Trinity*. Grand Rapids: Zondervan, 1988.

Metzger, Paul Louis, ed. *Trinitarian Soundings in Systematic Theology*. New York: T & T Clark, 2006.

Migliore, Daniel L. *Faith Seeking Understanding: An Introduction to Christian Theology*. Grand Rapids: Eerdmans, 1991.

Myers, A. C. *The Eerdmans Bible Dictionary*. Grand Rapids: Eerdmans, 1987.

Nee, Watchman. *The Normal Christian Life*. Wheaton, IL: Tyndale, 1977.

Oden, Thomas. *The Living God*. San Francisco: Harper & Row, 1987.

Packer, J. I. *Evangelism and the Sovereignty of God*. Downers Grove, IL: InterVarsity, 2008.

Phillips, J. B. *Your God Is Too Small*. New York: Macmillan, 1953.

Pinnock, Clark. *The Flame of Love*. Kindle ed. Downers Grove, IL: InterVarsity Press, 1999.

Prestige, G. L. *God in Patristic Thought*. London: SPCK, 1952.

Rahner, Karl. *The Trinity*. New York: Crossroad, 2005.

Richard of St. Victor. *Richard of St Victor*. Translated by Grover Zinn. New York: Paulist, 1977.

Roberts, Alexander, and James Donaldson, eds. *The Ante-Nicene Fathers*. Vol. 3. Grand Rapids: Eerdmans, 1976.

Sahms, Joseph. "Bravery of Angels and Men." *Hollywood Jesus*. n.d. http://www.hollywoodjesus.com/DVDDetail. cfm/i/05A38D11-FF0A-D937-6071B9085D619768/ ia/87A1C240-08C0-F07C-9730A7BECFC69D1F.

Sanders, E. P. *Paul and Palestinian Judaism: A Comparison of Patterns of Religion*. Minneapolis: Fortress, 1977.

Sawyer, M. James. *The Survivor's Guide to Theology*. Grand Rapids: Zondervan, 2006.

———. *A World Split Apart: Dualism in Western Culture and Theology*. Kindle ed. San Leandro, CA: Sacred Saga, 2014.

Schaff, Philip. *History of the Christian Church*. Vol. 3. Garland, TX: Galaxie Software, 2002.

————, ed. *The Nicene and Post-Nicene Fathers.* Vol. 7. Grand Rapids: Eerdmans, 1974.

————. *The Nicene and Post-Nicene Fathers, Second Series.* Vol. 4. Grand Rapids: Eerdmans, 1975.

Sloat, Donald. *Growing Up Holy and Wholly.* Brentwood, TN: Wolgemuth & Hyatt, 1990.

Smith, Kevin. *Dogma* (shooting script). n.d. http://www.imsdb.com/scripts/Dogma.html.

Taylor, John V. *The Go-Between God.* London: SCM, 2004.

Torrance, Thomas F. *Atonement: The Person and Work of Christ.* Edited by Robert T. Walker. Downers Grove, IL: InterVarsity Press, 2009.

————. *The Christian Doctrine of God: One Being, Three Persons.* Edinburgh: T & T Clark, 1996.

————. *The Doctrine of Jesus Christ.* Eugene, OR: Wipf & Stock, 2002.

————. *The Ground and Grammar of Theology.* New York: T &T Clark, 1980.

————. *Incarnation: The Person and Work of Jesus Christ.* Edited by Robert T. Walker. Downers Grove, IL: InterVarsity Press, 2008.

————. *The Mediation of Christ.* Colorado Springs, CO: Helmers and Howard, 1992.

————. *Theology in Reconstruction.* Grand Rapids: Eerdmans, 1965.

————. *The Trinitarian Faith.* Edinburgh: T & T Clark, 1997.

Waltke, Bruce K. *Creation and Chaos.* Portland: Western Seminary, 1975.

Walton, John. *The Lost World of Genesis One: Ancient Cosmology and the Origins Debate.* Downers Grove, IL: InterVarsity Press, 2009.

Warfield, B. B. *Biblical Doctrines.* Grand Rapids: Baker, 1980.

Webster, John. *Holiness.* Grand Rapids: Eerdmans, 2003.

White, James R. *The Forgotten Trinity: Recovering the Heart of Christian Belief.* Bloomington, MN: Bethany, 1998.

Widdicombe, Peter. *The Fatherhood of God from Origen to Athanasius.* Oxford: Clarendon, 1994.

Wood, D. R., and I. H. Marshall, eds. *New Bible Dictionary.* Leicester: InterVarsity, 1996.

Wright, N. T. *How God Became King: The Forgotten Story of the Gospels.* Kindle ed. New York: HarperCollins, 2012.

Young, Francis M. *From Nicaea to Chalcedon: A Guide to the Literature and Its Background.* Grand Rapids: Baker, 2010.

Young, William P. *The Shack.* Newbury Park, CA: Windblown Media, 2008.

Zizioulas, John D. *Being as Communion.* New York: St. Vladimir's Seminary Press, 1985.

Printed in the United States
By Bookmasters